# THE WORLD OF SCIENCE
# THROUGH THE MICROSCOPE

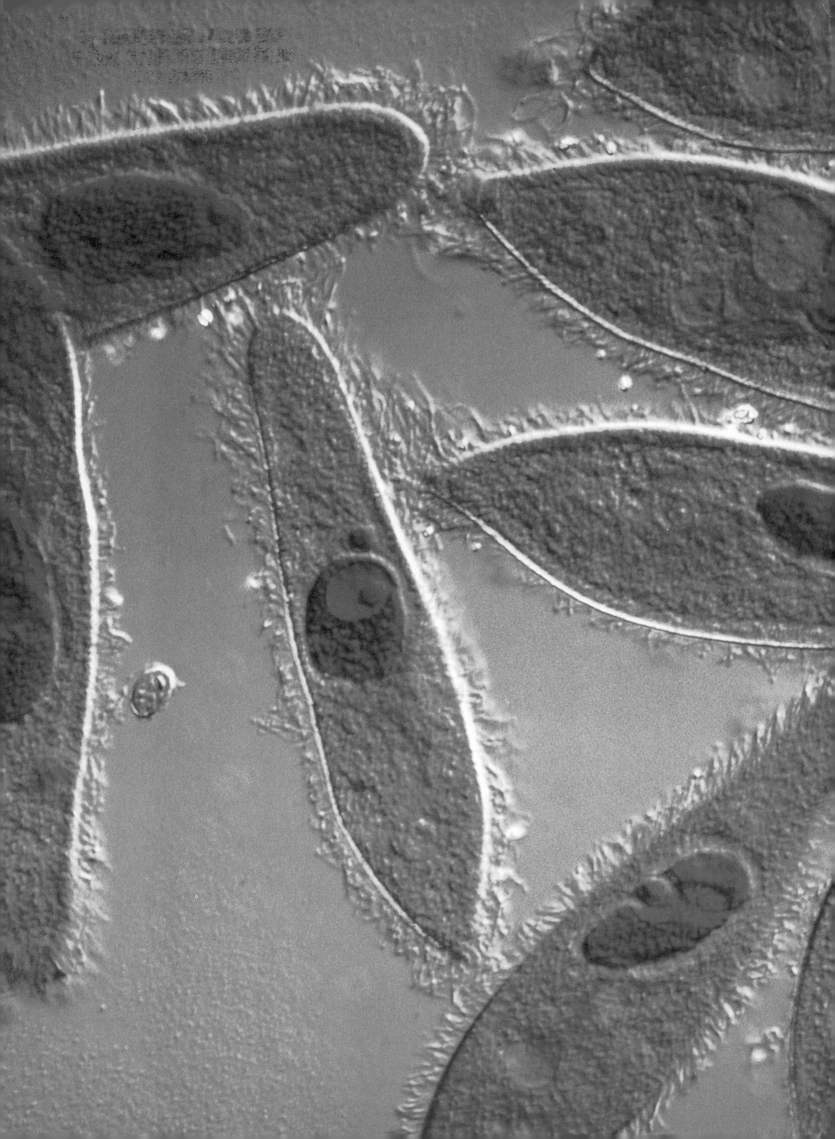

# THE WORLD OF SCIENCE
# THROUGH THE MICROSCOPE

## RON TAYLOR

**Facts On File Publications**
New York, New York • Bicester, England

First published in the United States of America in 1986
by Facts on File, Inc., 460 Park Avenue South, New
York, N.Y. 10016

First published in Great Britain in 1986 by Orbis
Publishing Limited, London

Copyright © 1986 by Orbis Publishing Limited, London

**Library of Congress Cataloging in Publication Data**

Main entry under title:
World of Science

Includes index.
Summary: A twenty-five volume encyclopedia of
scientific subjects, designed for eight- to twelve-year-olds.
One volume is entirely devoted to projects.
1. Science—Dictionaries, Juvenile.   1. Science—
Dictionaries
Q121.J86 1984      500      84-1654

ISBN 0-8160- 1075-7

Printed in Italy
10 9 8 7 6 5 4 3 2 1

**Consultant editors**
Eleanor Felder, Former Managing Editor, *New Book of
Knowledge*
James Neujahr, Dean of the School of Education, City
College of New York
Ethan Signer, Professor of Biology, Massachusetts
Institute of Technology
J. Tuzo Wilson, Director General, Ontario Science Centre

**Previous pages**
Seen through a
microscope that
magnifies many
hundreds of times, the
dark stained nucleus
and fringing hair-like
cilia of *Paramecium*
show up very clearly.

**Editor** Penny Clarke
**Designer** Roger Kohn

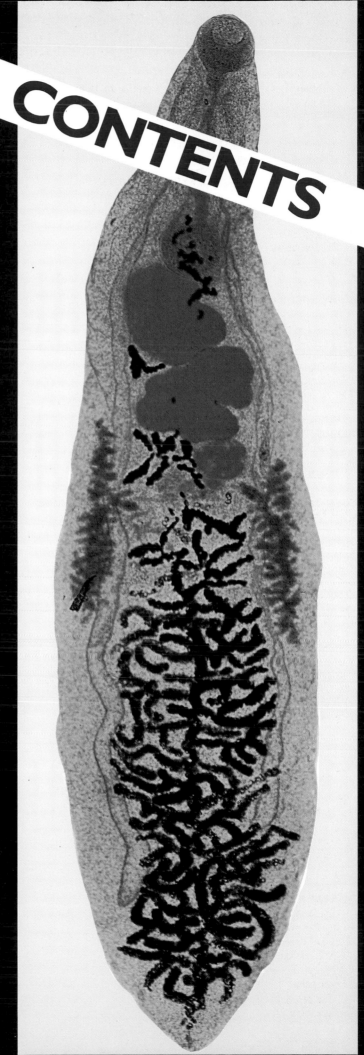

► This fluke can cause liver disease. Less than 2.5 cm (1 in) long, here it is magnified about 15 times.

# CONTENTS

## 1 THROUGH A MAGNIFYING GLASS

## 2 HUNTING WITH A MICROSCOPE

## 3 A CLOSER LOOK AROUND

## 4 MICROSCOPES, HEALTH AND DISEASE

## 5 THE GREATEST MAGNIFICATIONS

**Note** There are some unusual words in this book. They are explained in the Glossary on pages 62–63. The first time each word is used in the text it is printed in *italics*.

# I THROUGH A MAGNIFYING GLASS

## MAGNIFIED NATURE

◄Magnified about 4 times, a ladybird (or ladybug) climbs up a plantlet. Ladybirds are probably the best-known beetles, and besides being pretty, they do good in the garden by eating the plant pests called aphids. There are more kinds of beetles than any other insects, and many different kinds of ladybirds. You can easily tell these apart when you find them — especially if you look at them with a magnifying glass – because different ladybirds have different colours, usually red or yellow with black spots, and different numbers of spots. This one is a yellow 22-spot ladybird.

The world is a fascinating place, and the closer you look, the more fascinating it becomes. If you pay close attention to the smaller things and creatures around you, you will see that often they have quite intricate shapes and unexpected colours.

Your eyes alone can show you a great deal of this natural detail. Sometimes, though, many of the interesting or beautiful details will be just too small for you to make out clearly. Then, you will need to use an instrument such as a magnifying glass, to make the details look larger and clearer.

### Light and heat rays

A magnifying glass works by focussing, or concentrating, the rays of light that allow you to see things. If you have already used a magnifying glass to focus the Sun's rays, you will know that it concentrates heat rays as well as light rays. Perhaps you have set a piece of paper or some dry straw alight by this method.

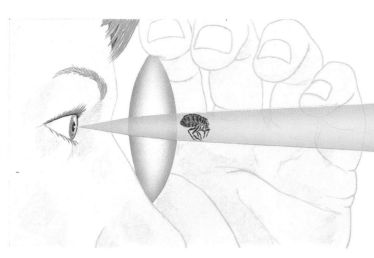

▼This photograph through a magnifying-glass shows baby opossums clinging to and feeding from their mother. Opossums look rat-like, but they are really *marsupials*, and related to such pouched mammals as kangaroos, wallabies and koalas. Unlike these Australian marsupials, opossums live in the USA and South America. Like those of their Australian relatives, opossums' babies are born very small indeed – about the size of a very small pea! Until they have grown up and developed considerably, as in this picture, they stay firmly attached to their mother's milk teats.

Destructive forest fires can be caused by a piece of glass, perhaps from a thrown-away bottle, acting as a magnifying glass to increase the power of the Sun's rays. This book, however, deals mostly with the more useful light-magnifying powers of magnifying glasses and microscopes. A magnifying glass, in fact, is a simple kind of microscope.

▲ What you see if you magnify a flea 10 times. The magnification is caused by light rays (by which you see the flea) bending as they pass through the lens, on the way to your eye.

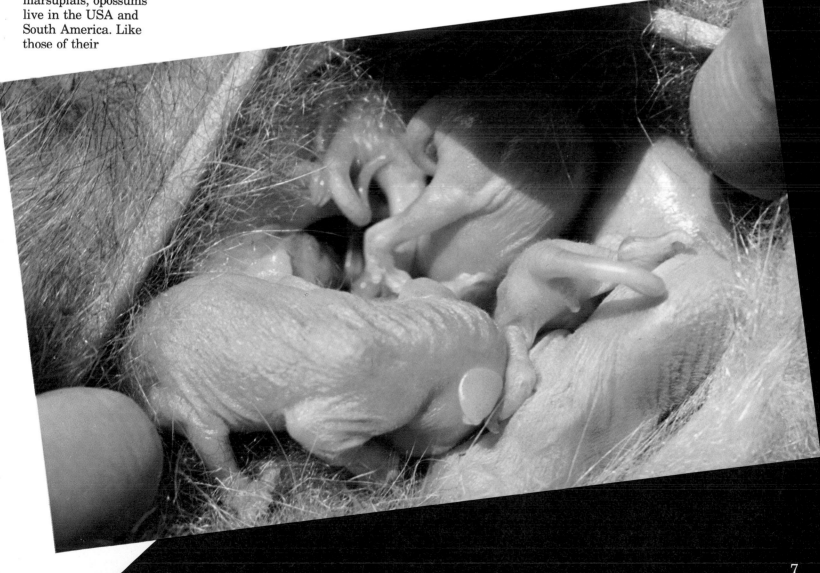

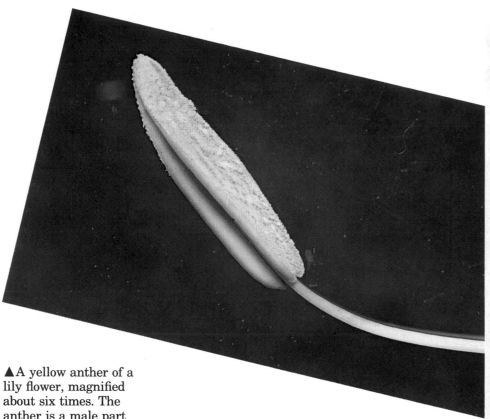

▲A yellow anther of a lily flower, magnified about six times. The anther is a male part of the flower, that holds pollen, which is shed by the anther when ripe, and floats off, or is carried off by insects, to fertilize another lily flower. At this low magnification the pollen grains appear as a yellow dust on the anther.

A strong magnifying glass will show you the world about five to ten times bigger than life-size. Such magnifying powers are quite strong enough to reveal hundreds of details you have never seen before, or else noticed only vaguely.

For example, outdoors in summer you may have admired the colours and patterns on the wings of the larger, more brilliant butterflies. A 5X magnifying glass (5X means five times) will at once show you equally beautiful decorations on the wings of smaller butterflies and moths that are usually hard to see.

**Busy midgets**
Brightly-coloured butterflies, flitting from flower to flower, are among the most noticeable and attractive creatures in nature, but they are by no means the most common.

Hidden in grasses, under sticks and stones, and in the soil itself, are countless numbers of small creatures, busily foraging for food. Usually, these creatures are far less brilliant than a big garden butterfly, but they have a fascinating range of shapes and movements, which can be seen through a magnifying glass.

▲Magnified about 10 times, this mosquito has just wriggled out of its pupa case, and is almost ready to make its first flight as an adult insect. This kind of mosquito has the scientific name *Culex pipiens*. On warm nights you may have heard its hateful little whine – or that of a near relative – close by your ear. Make no mistake – it is after your blood!

►Not a hairy caterpillar, but a leaf from one of the strange little plants called sundews, magnified about six times. These plants are insect-eaters that live in boggy places where nitrogen plant food is absent or in very short supply. Sundews get their nitrogen from the bodies of very small insects which they catch with the sticky hairs of their leaves. The hairs bend over quickly to trap the insect, after which its body is partly dissolved and absorbed by the plant.

▲The bumblebee is 10 times the size of the ant, which is 5 times the size of the springtail, which is 10 times the size of the microscopic mite.

◀Insects often lay their eggs and stick them to the undersides of leaves. In this magnified picture, caterpillars a centimeter or so long have hatched from their eggs.

▼Small shells picked up on the beach always repay magnification, because their shapes and patterns are then revealed in all their beauty. This collection includes the shells of small winkle-like animals, and coral.

# SMALL LIFE IN WATER

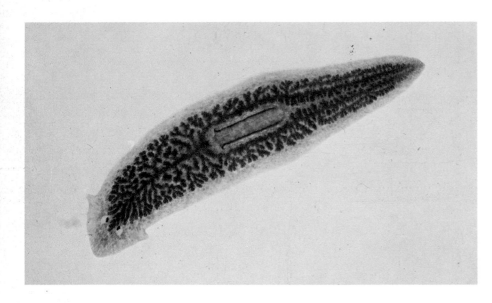

There are a host of small creatures that live in water. Puddles, ponds, rivers and lakes all teem with life, when conditions are suitable. The most important condition is enough food.

**Food and energy**

Since many small creatures eat live food, this means that an even greater number of still smaller creatures, their prey, also live in water.

Other small water creatures eat plant food. Tadpoles, one of the best-known small water creatures, nibble food plants – although frogs, which tadpoles grow into, catch live prey such as flies.

Water plants themselves manage to grow without the need for food, as we usually think of it. Green plants make most of their own body substances from the gas carbon dioxide. This gas is present everywhere in the air, and also dissolved in water. The plant needs three things to turn the gas into its own body substances. First it needs its own green colouring matter or pigment, called chlorophyll. Second it needs the energy of sunlight. Third, it needs water itself.

▲Planarians are small flatworms that swim about in streams by means of the beating of thousands of tiny hairs, or *cilia*, that cover their paper-thin bodies. A flatworm's mouth is in an unusual place – at the end of the tube you can see midway along this one's body.

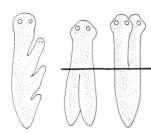

◄Planarian flatworms have another astonishing ability. If their bodies are cut, they can grow one or more extra heads or tails. Don't worry about the flatworms suffering – they can't feel pain, and sometimes reproduce simply by pulling apart into two halves.

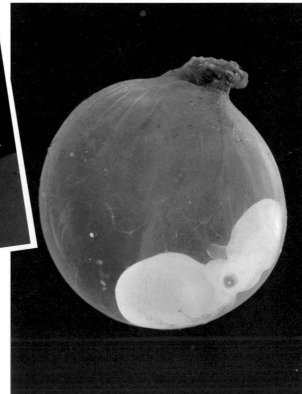

▲A strong magnifying glass will show you much more clearly what tadpoles look like, in this case, inside their toadspawn.

►The same magnifying glass, if you are lucky enough to live near a seaquarium, could show you this squidlet in its egg.

▼Sponges are the simplest of many-celled (multi-cellular) animals. They live mostly in the sea, though there are some freshwater sponges. Their blobby bodies often have little definite shape, though this one, for a reason you may be able to see, is called the purse sponge.

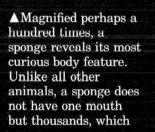

▲Magnified perhaps a hundred times, a sponge reveals its most curious body feature. Unlike all other animals, a sponge does not have one mouth but thousands, which cover the surface of its body. Through all these mouths the sponge draws water which contains the tinier forms of life on which it feeds.

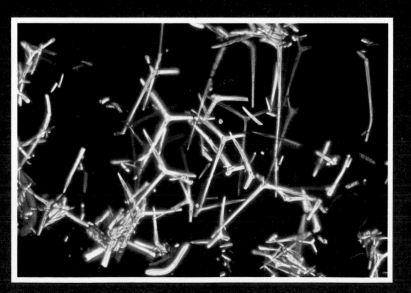

◀A sponge's body, unless it is encrusted with hard salts, is almost jelly-like in its softness. This needs a harder, stronger skeleton to make it more firm. In a sponge's body the skeleton takes the form of these microscopic *spicules*. Some sponges have chalky spicules, others have glassy or horny spicules.

# CORALS UP CLOSE

If you have been lucky enough to visit a tropical seaside place, you may know that a coral reef is one of the most brilliant and varied places on the sea bed. Not only the corals themselves, but also the fish swimming around and between them, are patterned in the most vivid colours.

Many of these brilliantly-coloured fish feed by nibbling the corals. Although some corals look rather like underwater plants, all corals are really animals. Corals are related to other sea animals such as jellyfish and sea anemones. A single mass of coral in a coral reef may be many yards across, but each of its coral animals is so small that it is clearly visible only through a magnifying glass.

Each tiny coral animal lives in its own area, which is just one small hole among thousands or millions of others in the chalky mass of coral. From its hole, the coral animal emerges to feed on still smaller creatures living in the warm water over the reef. But it does not come right out, because its soft body is connected to those of other coral animals all around it in the reef.

▲Vivid life on the coral reef. As bright and colourful as flowers, these little coral animals spread out their rays of tentacles to catch their microscopic prey, which lives in the sea water around them. The delicate tentacles are really fatal traps, because they are armed with thousands of stinging cells. Any prey creature unfortunate enough to brush against a tentacle is quickly stung and paralyzed. Then the tentacles together push the paralyzed prey into the mouth, situated at the centre of the tentacles.

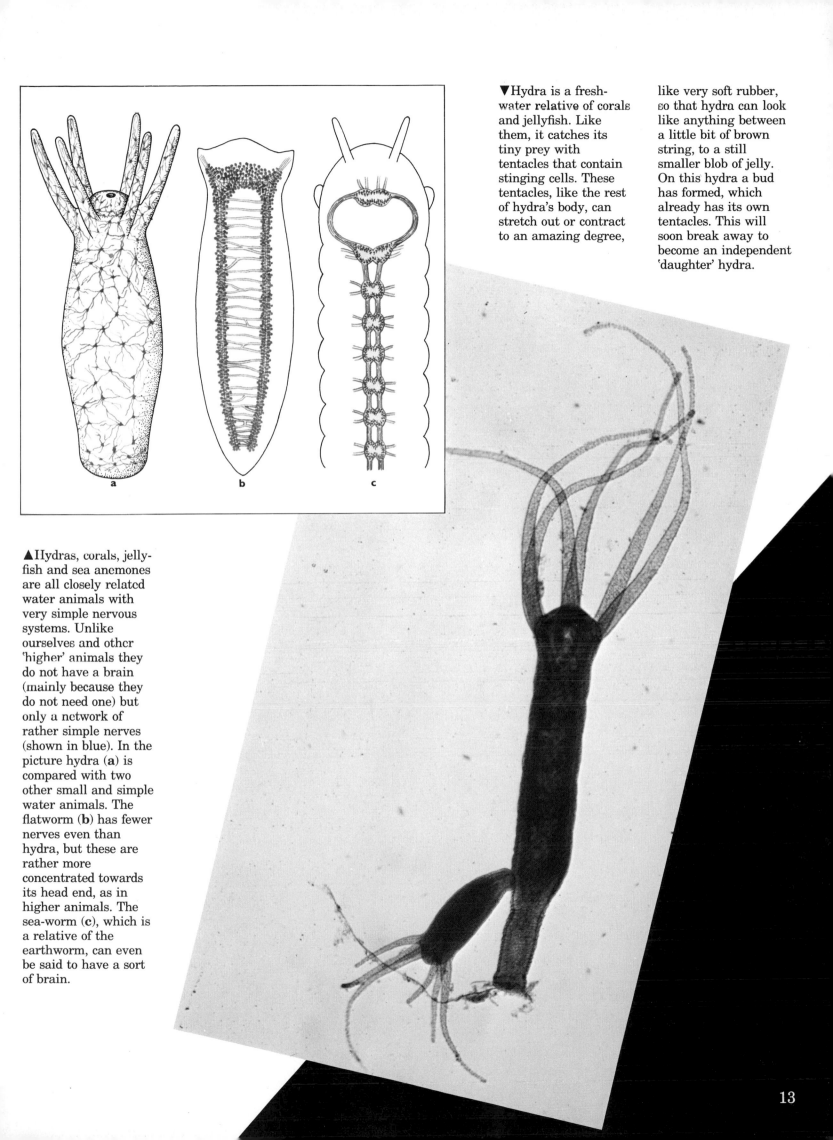

▼Hydra is a fresh-water relative of corals and jellyfish. Like them, it catches its tiny prey with tentacles that contain stinging cells. These tentacles, like the rest of hydra's body, can stretch out or contract to an amazing degree, like very soft rubber, so that hydra can look like anything between a little bit of brown string, to a still smaller blob of jelly. On this hydra a bud has formed, which already has its own tentacles. This will soon break away to become an independent 'daughter' hydra.

▲Hydras, corals, jelly-fish and sea anemones are all closely related water animals with very simple nervous systems. Unlike ourselves and other 'higher' animals they do not have a brain (mainly because they do not need one) but only a network of rather simple nerves (shown in blue). In the picture hydra (a) is compared with two other small and simple water animals. The flatworm (b) has fewer nerves even than hydra, but these are rather more concentrated towards its head end, as in higher animals. The sea-worm (c), which is a relative of the earthworm, can even be said to have a sort of brain.

▼Euglena is a microscopic, single-celled green alga that lives in pond and lake water. Although plant-like, it swims around by the lashing of its long whip or *flagellum*, always moving towards the light, which it detects with its red eyespot.

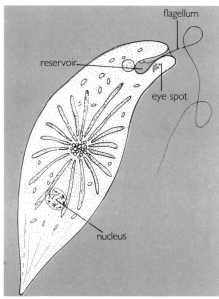

## STILL SMALLER LIFE

▼In the still, rather murky water of a pond or canal lurk many kinds of microscopic animals, two of which are shown below. Stentor is a trumpet-shaped protozoan or single-celled animal that feeds on even smaller pond creatures. Arcella (**inset**) is an amoeba relative. It has fed on two diatoms, which you can see inside its shell.

A magnifying glass will show you hundreds of new and fascinating details of the world around you — but a microscope will show you far, far more. What the microscope reveals is a whole new world that normally you cannot see at all.

In this microscopic world, creatures the size of a pin head are giants. Most creatures of the microscopic world are so small that a pin head would hold thousands or even hundreds of thousands of them.

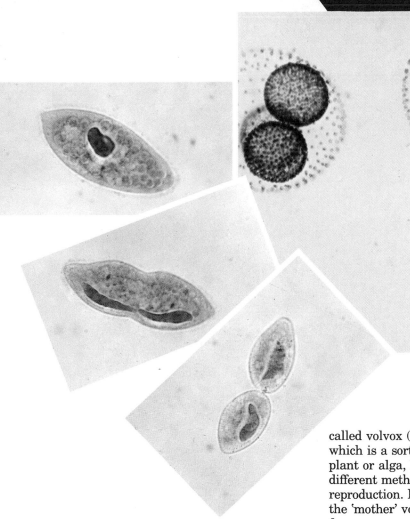

▼Stylonychia has only one cell but this is very complicated, being covered with hairs and bristles. Like paramecium, it is a member of the large group of protozoans called ciliates – cilia being another name for cell hair. Stylonychia scuttles around on its bristles, which are really many cilia fused together, searching for microscopic food.

▲How do the microscopic creatures that often swarm in water reproduce and multiply themselves? Paramecium (**above**) is a protozoan or single-celled animal that can reproduce simply by dividing in two. Its *nucleus*, also divides and is shared between the two 'daughter' cells. The ball of cells called volvox (**top**), which is a sort of green plant or alga, has a different method of reproduction. Inside the 'mother' volvox form many small 'daughter' balls of cells, which are eventually released and grow up to their full size – as huge, in the microscopic world, as the head of a pin!

Like our familiar, far larger world, the microscopic world has its animals and its green plants. Many of its animals, though, consist of only a single living cell. Our own bodies, by contrast, contain billions of living cells. Microscopic, one-celled animals are called *protozoa*, a word which means 'first animals'.

## Plants that swim
Many microscopic green plants also consist of only one living cell. Unlike the green plants of our larger world, some of these one-celled plants move around actively. Like many of the protozoa, or one-celled animals, they swim about freely from place to place.

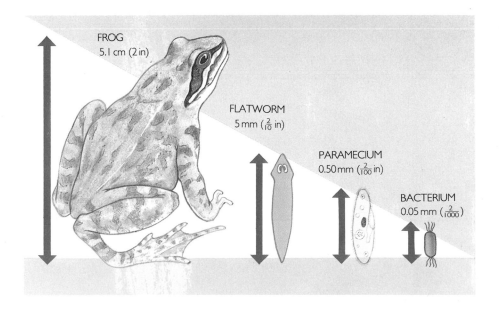

FROG
5.1 cm (2 in)

FLATWORM
5 mm ($\frac{2}{10}$ in)

PARAMECIUM
0.50 mm ($\frac{2}{100}$ in)

BACTERIUM
0.05 mm ($\frac{2}{1000}$)

▲Each creature is ten times smaller than the one to its left. The paramecium and the *bacterium* are so small that they can only be seen through the microscope.

# HUNTING THE AMOEBA

Ponds are fine places to look for microscopic life. A single drop of pond water, particularly when it comes from a weedy and perhaps rather smelly pond, often contains huge numbers of microscopic creatures. Looking through your microscope at such a rich drop of pond water, you may be confused at first by all the busy life going on.

Some microscopic creatures will whizz across the view or 'field' of the microscope so quickly that you can hardly tell what they look like. Usually these are *ciliates*, one-celled animals or protozoa. Other creatures swim about more slowly. These include many of the microscopic green plants.

If you patiently go on looking through your microscope, you might be lucky enough to spot an amoeba. This single-celled animal moves more slowly still, not by swimming but by 'flowing' about from place to place. A few kinds of amoeba are large enough to be spotted fairly easily, but most kinds are so small and transparent that they take some finding.

▼The world's biggest amoebas are somewhat larger than the head of a pin. The smallest amoebas are not much bigger than a pin-point.

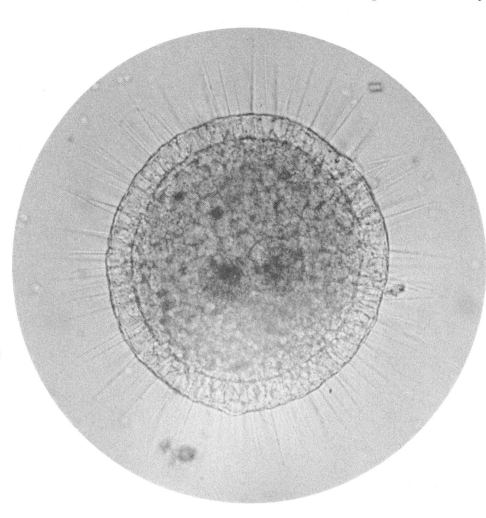

▼Some amoeba relatives make microscopic shells. Examples are these foraminiferans, whose shells may form deep *oozes* on the ocean bed.

◄Another amoeba relative is Actinosphaerium, which belongs for obvious reasons to the group known as sun animals or heliozoans. The rays of its tiny sun really serve a similar purpose to the blobby extensions or *pseudopodia* of the more familiar amoeba **opposite**. These rays are covered with moving *protoplasm* that traps still tinier creatures as food.

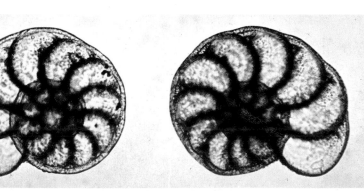

 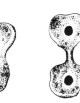

▲Amoebas, like many other single-celled creatures, reproduce themselves usually by simply dividing into two smaller cells, which then grow to the original size.

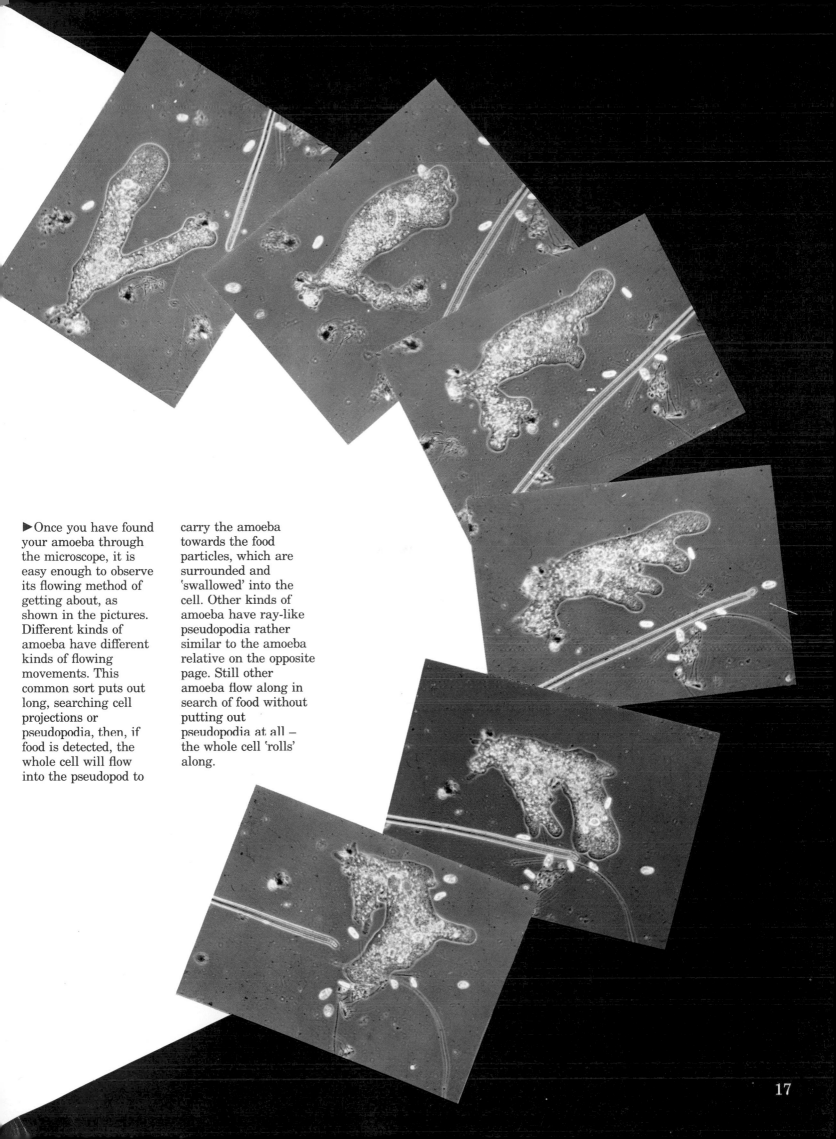

►Once you have found your amoeba through the microscope, it is easy enough to observe its flowing method of getting about, as shown in the pictures. Different kinds of amoeba have different kinds of flowing movements. This common sort puts out long, searching cell projections or pseudopodia, then, if food is detected, the whole cell will flow into the pseudopod to carry the amoeba towards the food particles, which are surrounded and 'swallowed' into the cell. Other kinds of amoeba have ray-like pseudopodia rather similar to the amoeba relative on the opposite page. Still other amoeba flow along in search of food without putting out pseudopodia at all – the whole cell 'rolls' along.

# MICROSCOPIC JUNGLES

Jungles are places where plant life is very plentiful, crowded and varied. In a thick tropical jungle such as the one around the River Amazon in South America, trees and other green plants of many different kinds all crowd together. A drop of water from a weedy pond, seen through the microscope, may show as crowded and varied plant life. It is a microscopic jungle.

**Threads, sheets and singles**
In the microscopic jungle, algae or simple green plants take the place of the great variety of plants in the Amazon jungle.

In place of big trees, the microscopic jungle has many long threads or *filaments* of living green cells. You will see these all tangled up together rather as jungle creepers twine around other plants.

Between the tangled green threads you will see other inhabitants of the microscopic jungle. These include smaller green threads and sheets of living cells, which take the place of jungle bushes and shrubs, and still smaller single-celled algae, which take the place of the flowers of the Amazon jungle.

▲A common member of the microscopic jungle is this green alga, called Ulothrix. It is here magnified about 100 times. Most types or species of ulothrix live in the still waters of ponds and slow-flowing rivers. Other species live in faster flowing streams or on the tidal parts of seashores, where they are prevented from being washed away by a sticky cell, or holdfast, at one end of their long filament. Each strand or filament contains a large number of similar green cells. The green is due to the same kind of chlorophyll pigment found in more complicated green plants.

▶Spirogyra is another green alga, very common in stagnant ponds where it forms slimy clumps and 'hairy' masses. The chlorophyll of ulothrix (**opposite**) is contained in each cell in a collar-shaped packet or *chloroplast*. In spirogyra the chloroplast has a delicate spiral shape. This is clearer in the spirogyra shown on page 22. In this picture, the cell contents of two spirogyra filaments have rounded up for mating or conjugating. Tubes have formed between several cells of the two filaments, through which the contents of one cell flows into and combines with that of the other. Each fertilized cell then grows into a new filament.

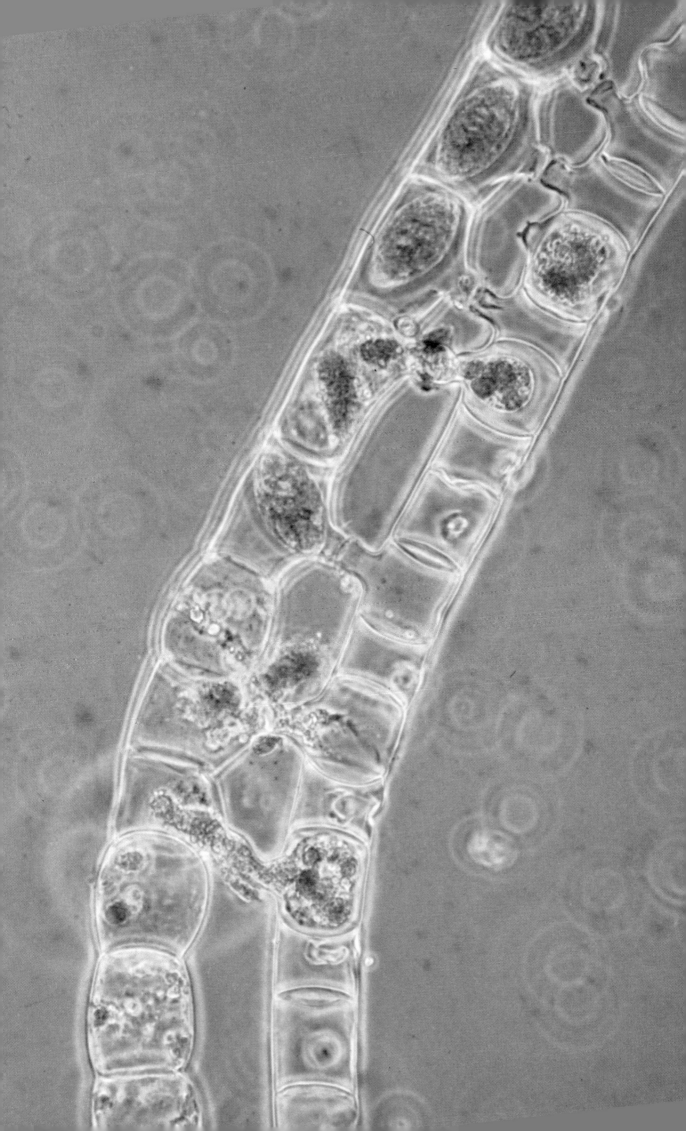

## Movements in the microscopic jungle

Unlike the plants of the Amazon jungle, many of the plants of the microscopic jungle move around from place to place. One sort of microscopic plant, Euglena, which swims around freely in a spiral or corkscrew motion, is shown on page 14.

In the green tangle of the microscopic jungle, most of the tangled threads cannot move, but some thread-like algae can move around, with a sort of gliding motion. The one you are most likely to see in a drop of pond water is called Oscillatoria. To 'oscillate' means to 'sway from side to side'. This is just how Oscillatoria moves along, with the first few cells of its long green filament swaying regularly. Then, for no apparent reason, its long thread may reverse its movement, making it travel in the opposite direction, when its other end will sway regularly from side to side.

## Diatoms

Diatoms are single-celled algae and some of them also move by gliding. Diatoms are not much like green plants to look at. They are often yellow rather than green in colour and their bodies are made of a hard, glass-like material, and are very regular in shape, though different kinds of diatom have different shapes.

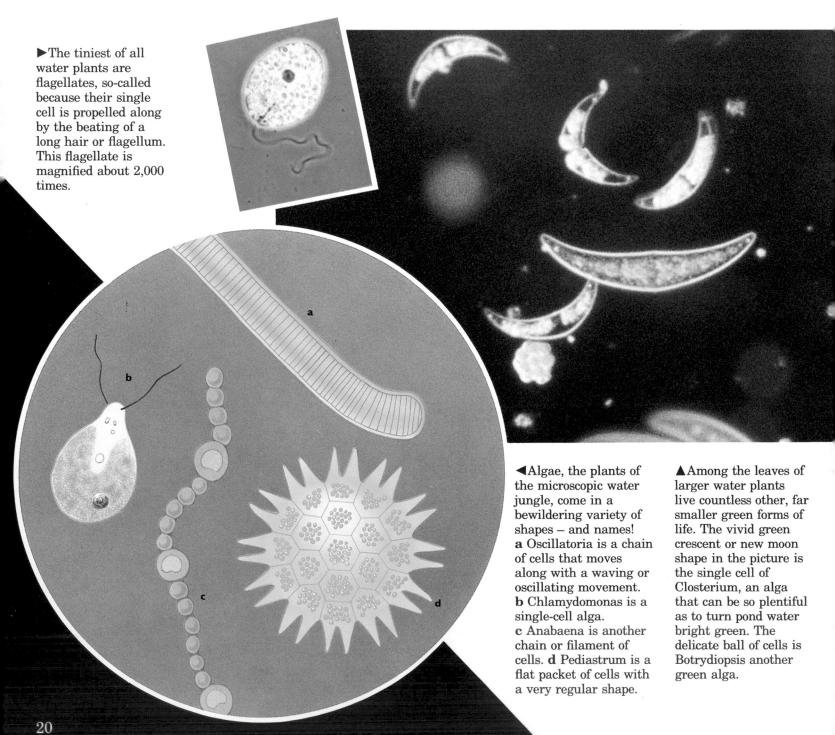

►The tiniest of all water plants are flagellates, so-called because their single cell is propelled along by the beating of a long hair or flagellum. This flagellate is magnified about 2,000 times.

◄Algae, the plants of the microscopic water jungle, come in a bewildering variety of shapes – and names!
**a** Oscillatoria is a chain of cells that moves along with a waving or oscillating movement.
**b** Chlamydomonas is a single-cell alga.
**c** Anabaena is another chain or filament of cells. **d** Pediastrum is a flat packet of cells with a very regular shape.

▲Among the leaves of larger water plants live countless other, far smaller green forms of life. The vivid green crescent or new moon shape in the picture is the single cell of Closterium, an alga that can be so plentiful as to turn pond water bright green. The delicate ball of cells is Botrydiopsis another green alga.

▼Diatoms are among the most plentiful of all microscopic water plants or algae. They are single-celled but often form long chains of cells, or stick to one another to make star- like or yet other shapes. You can see from the pictures that diatoms have very regular shapes. Basically they are of two shapes, long-bodied or round-bodied. In all diatoms the soft protoplasm is contained in a hard, glassy box – the shape that you see – which is marked or sculptured in intricate patterns. The diatoms in the lower right picture are rainbow-coloured because their glassy shells have split the light travelling through them into many beams of different coloured light.

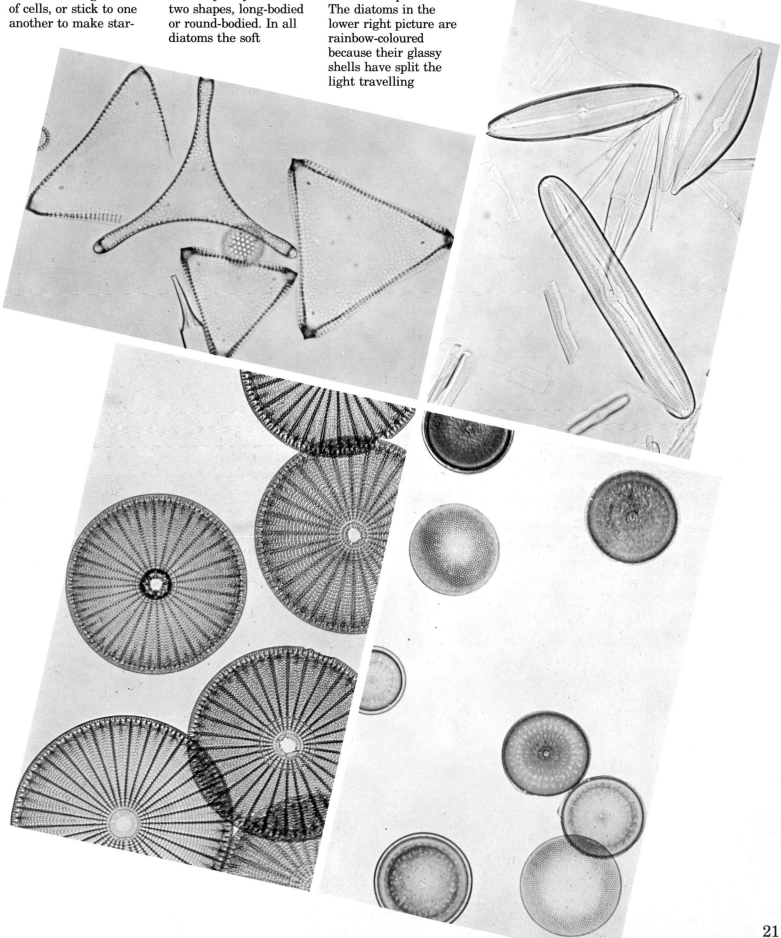

# MICROSCOPIC ZOOS

◀ Rotifers – seen here attached to a filament of spirogyra – are microscopic many-celled animals so common that any garden puddle or drain is likely to contain millions. Rotifers sweep their still-tinier prey into their mouths with a 'rotating' circle of hairs or cilia.

A zoo is a place where you can visit many different kinds of animal. So a microscopic zoo is a place in which you can see many different kinds of microscopic animal. Where can you find a microscopic zoo?

Once again, a drop of soupy green pond water is a very good place to look.

On some of the earlier pages in this book there are a number of microscopic pond-water animals. Most of these are single-celled animals or protozoa. Soupy green pond water swarms with these microscopic creatures, but it is also rich in animals which, like ourselves, have bodies composed of many living cells.

Of course, being so very small, the body of a microscopic animal cannot have billions of cells like that of a human being – there just isn't room for them all! The bodies of some microscopic animals have dozens of cells, others perhaps as many as a hundred or more.

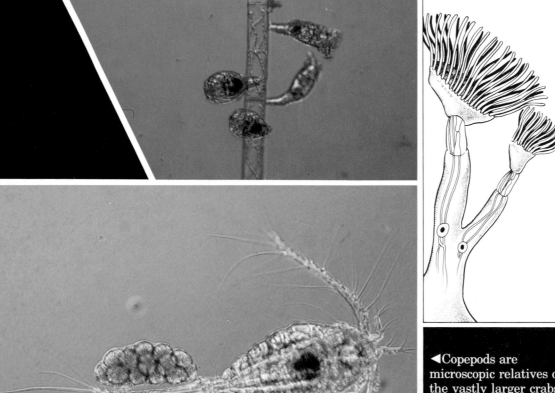

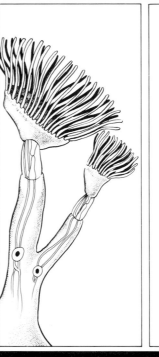

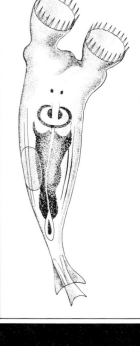

◀ Copepods are microscopic relatives of the vastly larger crabs and lobsters. They live in fresh water and also in incredible numbers in the oceans, Copepods are among the major sources of food for shoals of herring and other common fishes.

▲ Two microscopic-zoo animals that look rather alike but in fact are quite unrelated. On the **left** is Plumatella, a kind of moss animal. On the **right** is Philodina, one of many different kinds or species of rotifer.

## Microscopic relatives

Tiny as they are, many of these pond-water creatures have well-known relatives in our larger world. Some are microscopic cousins of the much larger earthworms. 'Water fleas' such as Daphnia are relatives of lobsters and crabs – which may be a million times bigger! However, some of the commonest of pond-water animals, such as rotifers and hairybacks, seem to have no close relatives at all.

◄Hairybacks or gastrotrichs are microscopic animals about the same minute size as rotifers (**opposite**). Like rotifers, they do not seem to be closely related to any other microscopic or larger animals.

▼Earthworms too have their microscopic relatives. This fresh-water annelid worm is only about 0.25 mm ($\frac{1}{100}$ inch) long, as shown by the green Volvox alga it has swallowed.

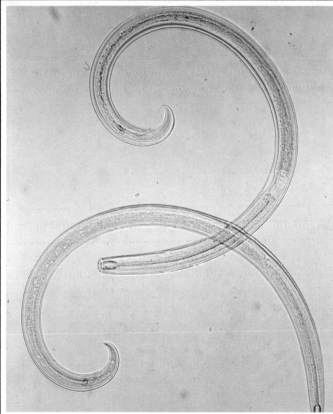

▲Microscopic roundworms or eelworms are the commonest animal parasites of plants. They exist in such huge numbers that if all the rest of nature were to disappear, the eelworms would form 'ghosts' of all the world's vegetation!

►Daphnia, or the water flea, is another microscopic crab relative. It is common in fresh water and is widely used as a fish food in home aquaria. Daphnia jigs around by jerking movements of its long antennae.

# A CLOSER LOOK AROUND

Mites are relatives of spiders, many of them so small that they are only visible through a magnifying glass or a microscope. The house mite (**left**) is shown among particles of dust, so you can see how small the mite must be. Mites can cause us a great deal of trouble. Some bore into the human skin and lay their eggs there, producing a severe irritation. Others cause the disease mange in our domestic pets, particularly cats, in which it can be fatal. The tiny house mite is not so vicious, but may be an important cause in some people of the distressing shortness of breath known as asthma. The picture (**above**) shows a house mite at much greater magnification still. It was taken with an electron microscope (see page 56).

# AROUND YOUR HOME

### Dusty deserts

Microscopic life can be found in houses as well as in ponds. Even the best-cleaned house has some dust in it, and a bit of dust from behind a picture or a crack in a floorboard, may well contain one or two house mites or other microscopic creatures. Almost certainly the dust will contain larger numbers of bacteria. These single-celled forms of life are common everywhere, but they are so small that they cannot be seen without a powerful microscope.

But if pond water contains crowded microscopic jungles, then house dust is more like a microscopic desert. It has very little moisture – and water is vital to all forms of life. Still, some life occurs in even the driest desert, because the creatures living there are careful not to lose the water they carry about in their bodies.

Animals who live in large sandy deserts are usually small creatures who make burrows to stay out of the Sun and so avoid losing body-water. Inhabitants of household dust are, of course, far smaller still, so they can survive by storing even smaller amounts of vital water.

### Watery larders

Unlike dusty household nooks and crannies, bathrooms and kitchens are never short of water, so you might expect more kinds of small or microscopic creatures to try to find homes there.

They often succeed in doing so, even when the rooms in question are kept as clean as possible. A spider has a way of suddenly appearing in even the cleanest bath. It has fallen in there while looking for flies – which may also haunt the bathroom in warm weather. Someone who takes pride in their clean home may be horrified to find cockroaches in the kitchen. But any food carelessly left out in the kitchen or elsewhere may soon attract household pests such as cockroaches or mice. Even more certainly it will attract those widespread feeders, the moulds or fungi, whose microscopic spores are about everywhere. That is why moulds can develop so amazingly swiftly on, for example, stale bread.

▲A magnifying glass may show you one or more of these in your bathroom or kitchen! The silverfish is a small wingless insect that feeds on almost any bits of food you drop, and failing this, will even chew the paste under the wallpaper! The silver-fishes' relatives, also small and harmless, live mostly among dead grasses and fallen leaves. It is easy to see why they are called Bristletails.

▼The two pictures show microscopic views of two fabrics that are very common about the house and in your clothes. The rougher, more uneven strands are those of cotton fibres. The smoother, glistening, more even network is composed of synthetic fibres, of which you can see two kinds of different thicknesses woven together.

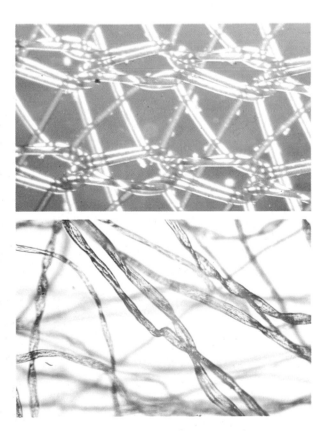

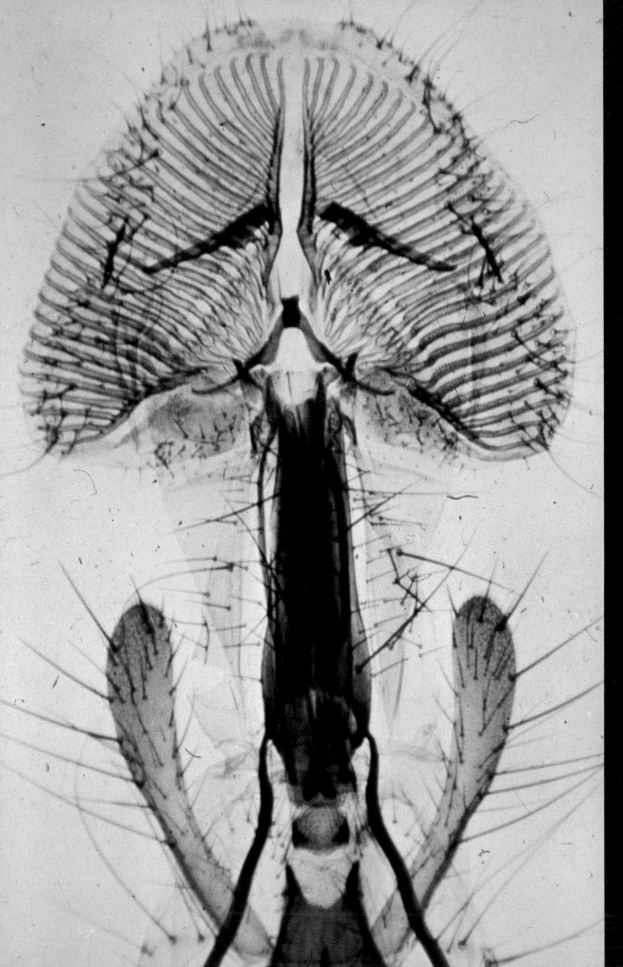

◄This *photomicrograph* or photograph taken through a microscope, shows the tongue and some other mouth parts of a blowfly, magnified about 200 times. The blowfly (or bluebottle or greenbottle) mops and sucks up its liquid food with this complicated tongue or *proboscis*. The food may be nectar from flowers, or less pleasantly, liquids oozing from the bodies of dead and putrefying animals, in which the blowfly also lays its eggs. Blowflies have a really important function in helping to get rid of dead bodies. Unfortunately some also feed from, and lay their eggs in, the bodies of living animals, causing troublesome sores.

►Fungi are plant-like organisms common about the house and garden – and almost everywhere else except, perhaps, the sea. You probably know the fungi, mushrooms and toadstools growing in soil or on larger plants. Most fungi, though, are microscopic in size. This picture shows the common black fungus mould Aspergillus, magnified almost 1,000 times. This mould, together with the even commoner green Penicillium mould, often grows on food left lying around. Fungi spread themselves mainly by their very tiny spores, of which they make huge numbers. You can see the black spore heads or sporangia of Aspergillus in the picture. Each one contains hundreds of spores, which float off in the slightest wind – perhaps to land on food in your kitchen!

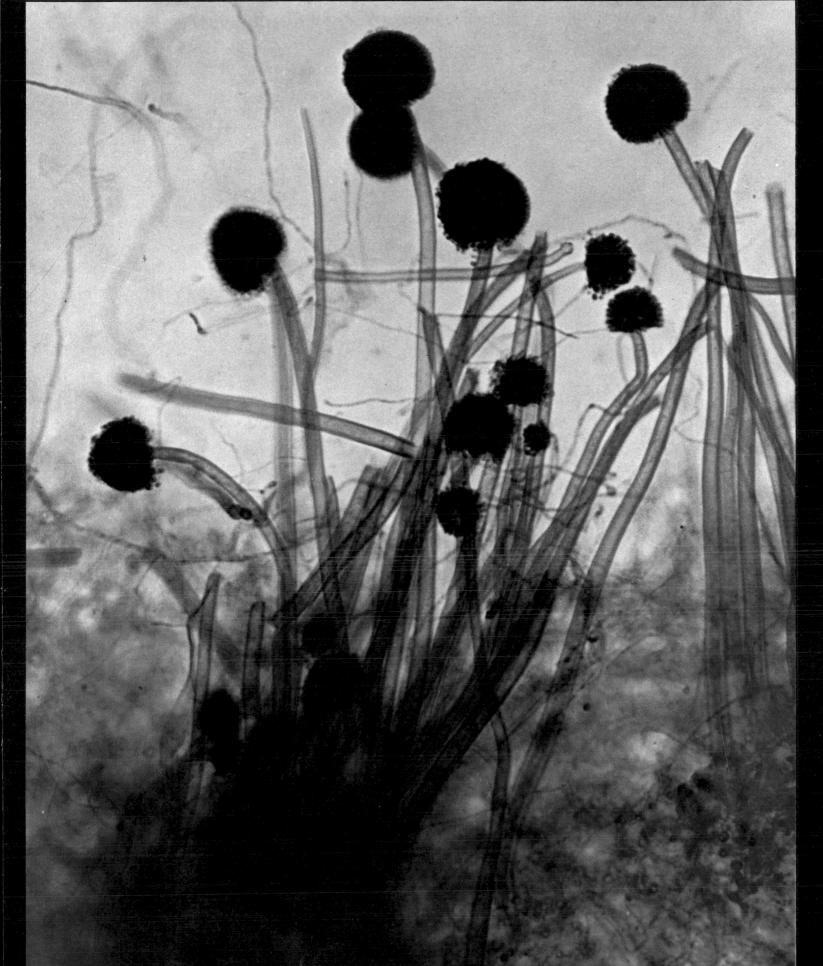

▶If you shake a flower it may give off a cloud of pollen. Under the microscope, pollen grains from various flowers appear as one or more living cells, surrounded by a tough coat which sometimes has an attractive shape. To make them show up more clearly, these pollen grains have been stained with coloured dyes.

▲When a pollen grain reaches another flower, it sticks to the flower's central stigma and soon grows a tube down into the flower's ovary. Through this tube the flower is fertilized by the pollen grain, to produce a seed. If you catch a pollen grain and put it in weak sugar solution (sugar and water mixed), it grows a tube as in this picture.

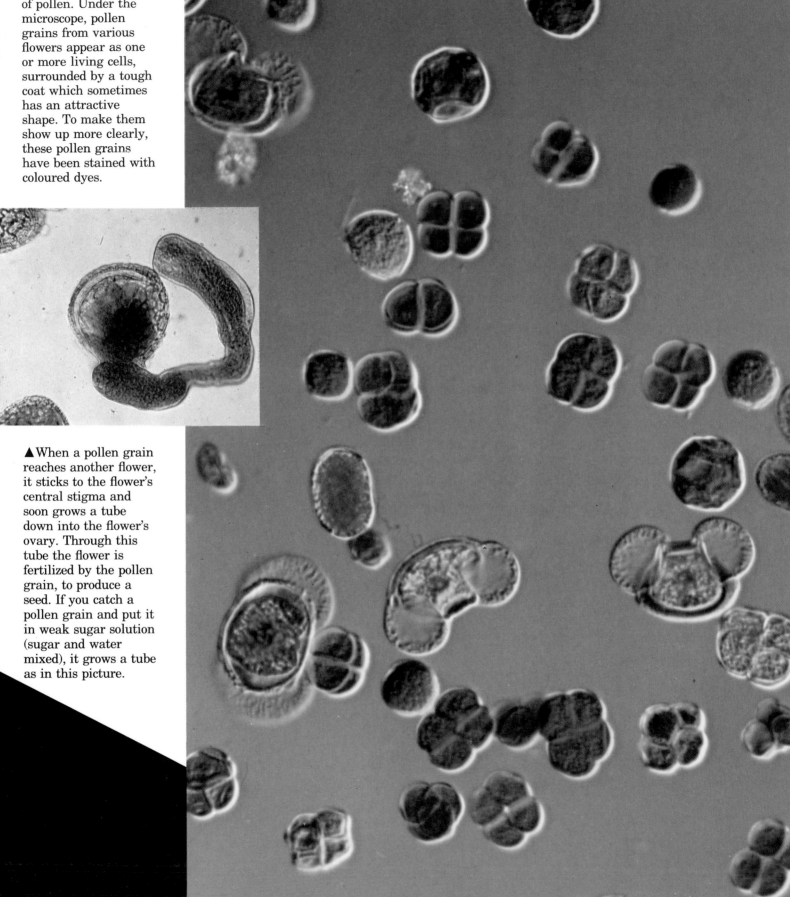

Gardens of all places are famous for being full of life. Birds, butterflies, bees and flowers are examples of the life we associate with gardens. Much less familiar, but even more plentiful, is the life hidden in garden soil and vegetation. The creatures and plants that live here are in general small and often microscopic in size, but their numbers are enormous.

Turn over any small pile of dead grasses or fallen leaves and you will find the little creatures that are living or sheltering there. Many of these will be tiny, wingless insects, the commonest of which are the springtails. These live not only under garden litter but also in soil and on water. You may have noticed them springing about on the surface of a pond in warm weather.

As for microscopic garden plants, most of these are well hidden, although a few are obvious enough. The green colour of many tree trunks is caused by millions of microscopic green algae, that live on the damper, shadier sides of the trunks.

▲*Pollination* of our most prized plants, including wheat shown here, can't always be left to nature and chance. Market gardeners and horticulturalists are expert in transferring pollen from one plant to another. In this way, new and better varieties of plant are produced.

sunlight    sunlight

carbon dioxide + water    light absorbed by chlorophyll    sugar + oxygen

water from roots

oxygen out carbon dioxide in

stoma

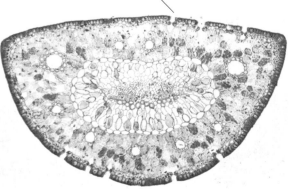

◀A pine needle, sliced across very thin, stained, and put under the microscope **left**. Compare it with the diagram **above**, to see how a leaf makes food substances for the plant. The leaf needs the gas carbon dioxide from the air. This enters the leaf through small holes called *stomata* (singular stoma). Inside the green leaf cells, the carbon dioxide reacts chemically with water to make sugary food substances. This reaction needs energy from sunlight, which is absorbed by the green plant pigment called chlorophyll.

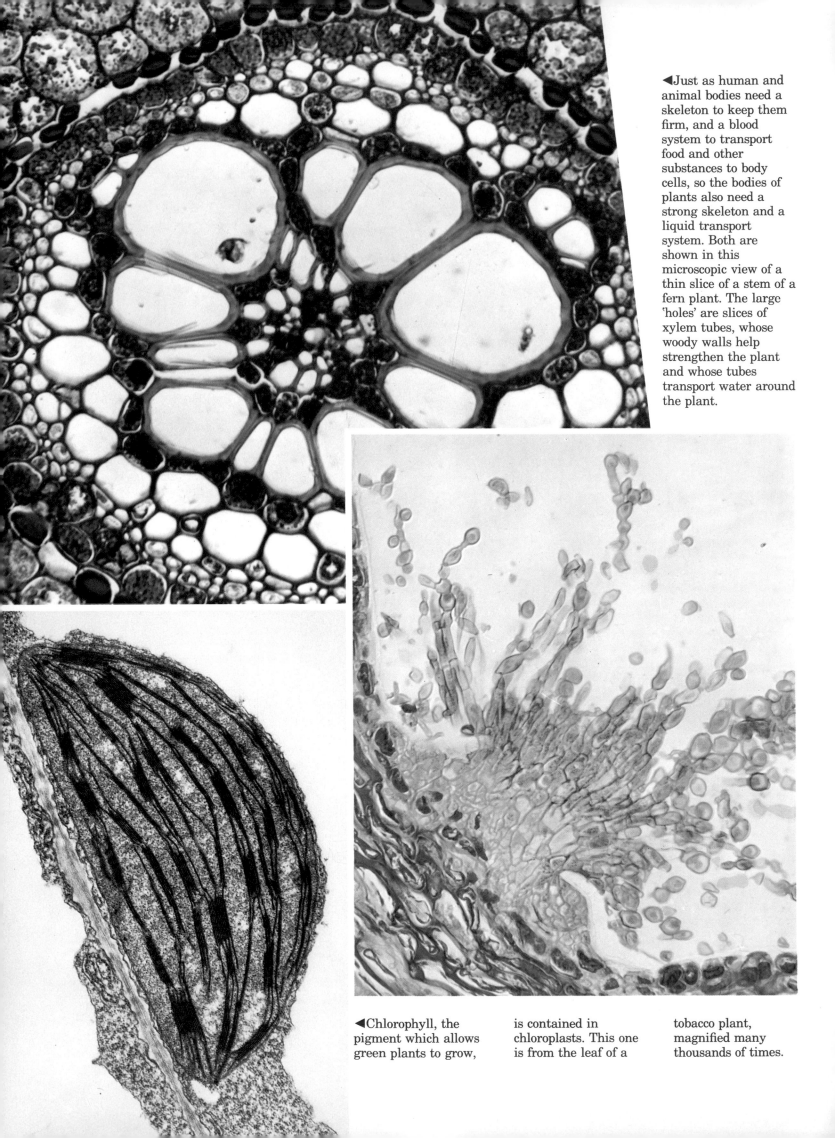

◄Just as human and animal bodies need a skeleton to keep them firm, and a blood system to transport food and other substances to body cells, so the bodies of plants also need a strong skeleton and a liquid transport system. Both are shown in this microscopic view of a thin slice of a stem of a fern plant. The large 'holes' are slices of xylem tubes, whose woody walls help strengthen the plant and whose tubes transport water around the plant.

◄Chlorophyll, the pigment which allows green plants to grow, is contained in chloroplasts. This one is from the leaf of a tobacco plant, magnified many thousands of times.

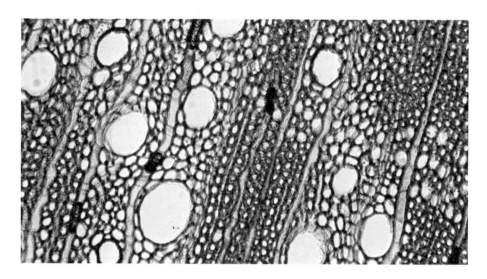

▶In this photomicrograph of a thin slice of oak wood, you can also see the holes of xylem tubes. But in this much bigger and heavier plant, the thick-walled woody tubes are more plentiful. Much more water and food has to be transported in an oak tree, which also needs a much stronger woody skeleton.

## Microscopic fungi

In gardens, meadows and woodlands you will often find fungi growing. Mushrooms and toadstools are the biggest fungi, and are easy to spot. A closer look at any piece of damp, dead wood – for example, a fallen tree – will probably reveal smaller fungi, some brightly coloured, although no fungus has the green colour typical of more advanced plants such as trees.

What are the small fungi doing on the damp wood? The answer is that they are feeding on it, rotting it down to simpler substances which pass into the soil. Without fungi, the world would be cluttered up with dead wood!

If you have a magnifying glass with you, look through it at where the fungus joins the wood and you may be able to see a mass of threads, each much finer than a human hair. These are not roots as in a higher plant, but are the true body of the fungus itself, as it stretches, mostly hidden, deeper inside the wood. The mushroom or other 'plant' that sticks up from wood or soil is just the spore carrier of the fungus. A fungus makes spores in the same way that a higher plant makes seeds. Spores, though, are so tiny that you need a powerful microscope to see them.

▼Ergot of rye is a fungus parasite of plants that can be fatally dangerous to animals and human beings. The three ears of rye (**below**) show the blackening caused by this fungus. Seen through the microscope (**far left**) is a single stroma of the ergot fungus, which contains many little oval packets of fungal spores. If any of the blackened rye ears, containing millions of spores, gets into rye bread, it can cause fatal poisoning.

◀Fungi are among the worst parasites of plants. In this photomicrograph, cells of a parasitic fungus are seen bursting out between the larger, flatter cells of the bark of an infected plant. The fungus is also releasing spores which float off down wind, perhaps to infect another plant. The fungus is not really green – only plants that are not parasites are green – it has been stained green so it shows up better.

### Plankton

Microscopic life abounds in the oceans. Floating in the sea is a 'living soup' of microscopic animals and plants, called the plankton. This is not easy to see, but there is more of it, in fact, than the total weight, or mass, of all animals and plants on dry land.

Plankton extends over huge stretches of the oceans, which cover seven out of every ten parts of the Earth's surface. Plankton, in fact, is the main foodstuff of the sea. It feeds the smaller fishes and other sea creatures, which are then prey for larger sea animals. Without plankton, the rich strange and varied life of the sea would cease to exist.

### Life based on sulphur

Even stranger than deep-sea fishes and squids are creatures that live on the deepest parts of the sea bed. These include giant worms, up to 2 m (6 ft) long, that feed on microscopic bacteria. The bacteria themselves feed on sulphur gases belching from deep cracks in the sea bed, which reach down to still deeper, hotter parts of the Earth's crust.

▼Sailors are familiar with wonderful night-time displays of luminescence in the surface layers of the oceans. These 'cold fire' displays may go on as far as the eye can see, yet they are caused by single-celled creatures of microscopic size, such as Noctiluca.

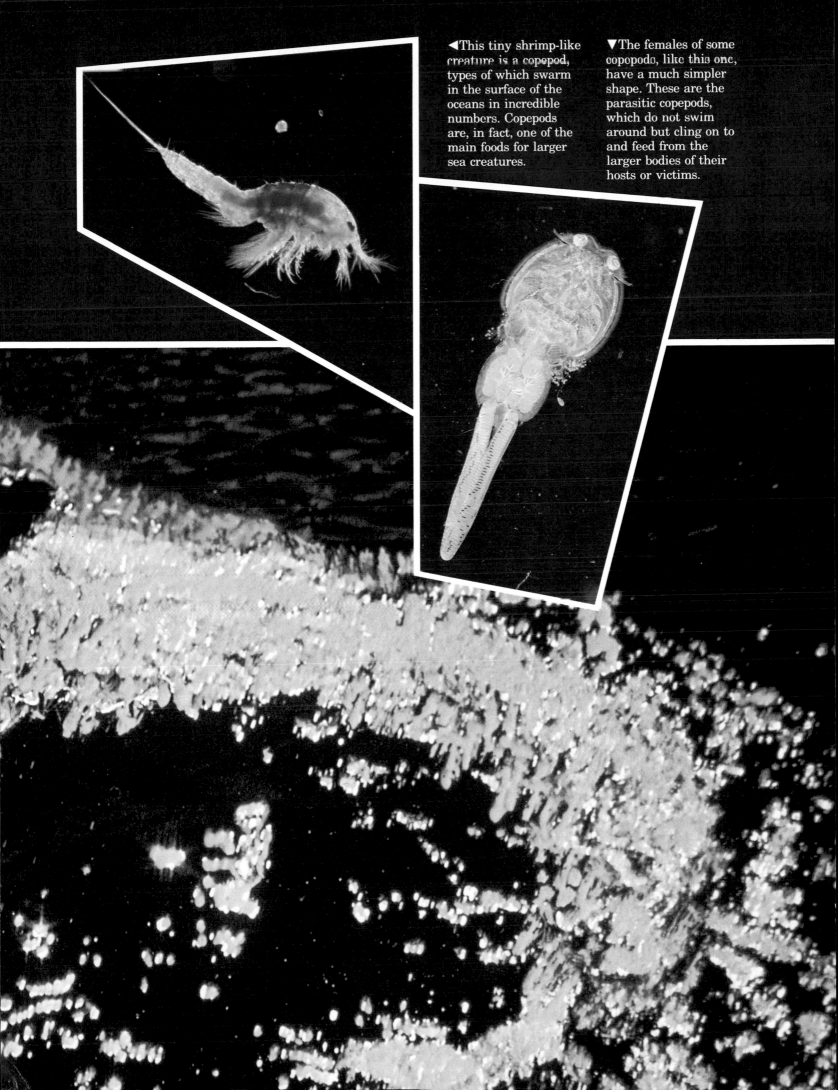

◄This tiny shrimp-like creature is a copepod, types of which swarm in the surface of the oceans in incredible numbers. Copepods are, in fact, one of the main foods for larger sea creatures.

▼The females of some copepods, like this one, have a much simpler shape. These are the parasitic copepods, which do not swim around but cling on to and feed from the larger bodies of their hosts or victims.

So far in this book we have looked mainly at the living world through the microscope. What about all the rest – the rocks, metals and other non-living substances? Is there a microscopic world to be discovered here, too?

## Microscopic minerals

The answer, of course, is 'Yes'. In fact, a whole branch of microscopic science is concerned with how non-living things, such as the minerals dug up from the Earth's crust, look under the microscope.

Nearly always, these minerals are made up of *crystals*. Sometimes the crystals are big enough to be obvious – gemstones or jewels are beautiful examples. More often, though, mineral crystals are microscopic in size. Metal crystals in particular are usually so small that the metal looks quite smooth or shiny, even though it is really made up of crystals.

The kinds of microscopic crystals in a mineral, and how they are arranged, often tell the scientist how the mineral was formed in the Earth's crust. They also give clues as to the useful properties of the mineral, for example its hardness and strength.

▲This tray of uncut diamonds has been magnified slightly to show the different colours and sizes of these precious stones. The most priceless diamonds of all are large, have plenty of sparkle but no colour. Smaller and darker diamonds are mostly used in industry for their cutting power – diamonds being the hardest of all substances. You may have seen someone cutting window glass with a diamond tool. More precious diamonds are made into gems by being cut (with other diamonds) into the regular shapes familiar in engagement rings and other jewels.

▲Diamond crystals (**above**) are made up of a single type of atom, carbon – also familiar as non-precious soot! The smaller, more feathery crystals (**left**) are those of the drug aspirin, a more complex chemical.

◄Metal crystals are usually much smaller than such familiar crystals as those of sugar and salt. The microscope shows metallurgists full details of the crystal structure of a metal or the metal mixtures called *alloys* – such as the silicon-iron alloy in the picture. This is of the greatest importance where a metal or alloy is being used to carry great weight or stress, because any flaws in the crystal structure can make a metal part weak and vulnerable – not a good thing if it is used as part of a high bridge or an airplane's wing.

▶A magnified view of another world – the picture shows crystals of a moon rock brought back to Earth in the early 1970s by US astronauts of the Apollo Project. To the naked eye, a lump of moon rock doesn't look as colourful as this. The photomicrograph gets its colours because it has been taken using polarized light, that is, light which vibrates only in one direction, or plane, and not in all planes like ordinary light. This causes 'interference effects' in different types of crystal, which to our eyes means that the crystals become vividly coloured.

# MICROSCOPIC INDUSTRY

Most of the things that we use in our daily lives are made in factories. Usually these need to be tested scientifically before we use them, to show that they are safe and well-made. Microscopes are often used for this purpose, for example to check on plastic fibres that are woven into cloth, or to examine metals and alloys for use in machines or other structures.

Sometimes the parts themselves are so small that they need to be made, as well as examined, by looking through the microscope. The tiny but complicated electrical circuits of pocket calculators and larger computers are good examples.

## Living industry

Some industries use microscopic forms of life to make their products. Beer, wine and vinegar are made using yeasts, which are microscopic forms of fungi. Baker's yeast, for example, is used to make bread.

These are ancient industries – people have been making beer, wine and bread for thousands of years. But industries of the future will use more and more *microbes*, or microscopic forms of life, to make new products. Already, many of our most valuable medical drugs are made by specially-grown microscopic fungi or bacteria. By the year 2000, other special microbes will also be used to grow better food crops and to make new kinds of industrial materials.

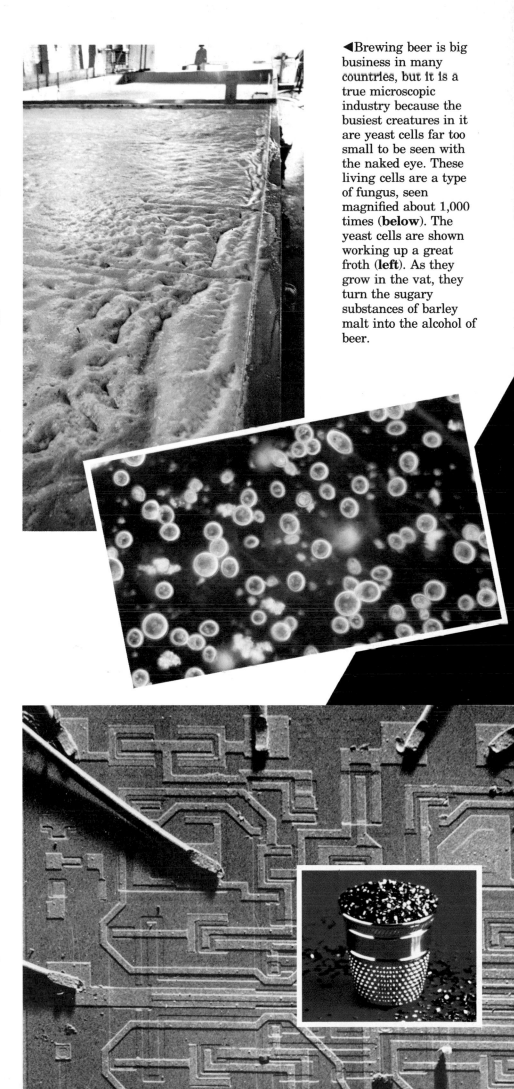

◀Brewing beer is big business in many countries, but it is a true microscopic industry because the busiest creatures in it are yeast cells far too small to be seen with the naked eye. These living cells are a type of fungus, seen magnified about 1,000 times (**below**). The yeast cells are shown working up a great froth (**left**). As they grow in the vat, they turn the sugary substances of barley malt into the alcohol of beer.

◀Microscopic view of a pair of tights! The picture shows woven strands of the synthetic fibre nylon, highly magnified with the electron microscope (page 56). Even when highly magnified, nylon fibre looks quite smooth, without any of the irregularity of natural fibres such as wool and cotton (page 25). Only natural silk can match the smoothness of synthetic fibres such as nylon, which explains the silky feel of all these materials.

▶Computers have their microscopic secrets, the extremely tiny electrical circuits that go to make up their memory and other systems. The large picture, also taken with an electron microscope, shows a complicated 'integrated circuit', countless thousands of which may go into a single computer. The thimbleful of 'chips' (**inset**) shows just how small these circuits are – and computer scientists are making them smaller every year.

# 4 MICROSCOPES, HEALTH AND DISEASE

## YOUR BODY THROUGH THE MICROSCOPE

▼With every breath you take in dust and other particles from the air, some of which could be irritating or harmful. This photomicrograph shows how your throat deals with such particles. The outside layer of throat cells have hairs or cilia. As these cilia beat, they drive mucus or slime, made by cells deeper in the throat, in an upward direction. Most inhaled particles are trapped in this mucus and then are harmlessly swallowed. Few get through to harm your lungs.

With a magnifying glass you can take a new look at your body. For example, you can see how each body hair enters the skin through its hair-hole or follicle. Also you will notice that your skin, between its hairs, is rough, rather like corrugated cardboard.

The outside of your body looks like this at a magnification of only 5X (five times). A more powerful microscope will magnify up to at least 500X – then the hair follicle will look as wide as a drain hole, and your hair as thick as a cable (page 41)!

Looking inside your body with a microscope is more difficult, although scientists have found ways of doing it. But you can easily obtain a small drop of your blood – by pricking your skin with a *clean* needle. When you smear this drop thinly on a glass slide, then examine it at a magnification of about 500X, you will see large numbers of your blood cells. Most of these will be the doughnut-shaped red blood cells. A few will look larger and more unevenly shaped. These are the white blood cells.

▼A picture of blood cells magnified more than 1,000 times. Among the roundish red cells which carry oxygen in the blood, is a larger white cell (but stained blue) called a phagocyte. This has the important task of gobbling up foreign particles such as bacteria, so helping to prevent disease.

►Many of our nerve cells have long tails or *axons* that reach to connect with other nerve cells or with an organ such as a muscle. The small picture shows a microscopic slice across an axon. The inner nerve fibre is surrounded by a wrapping of myelin, which acts like rubber insulation around an electric wire.

►The big picture shows a microscopic slice of part of the human cerebellum, that part of the brain that automatically controls how we stand up, walk and maintain our balance. The nerve cells are not magnified as much as in the smaller picture. They appear most clearly as dots and lines in the yellow-stained areas.

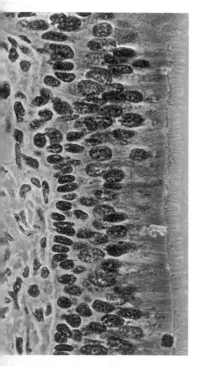

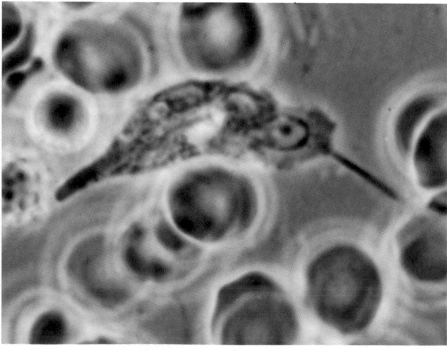

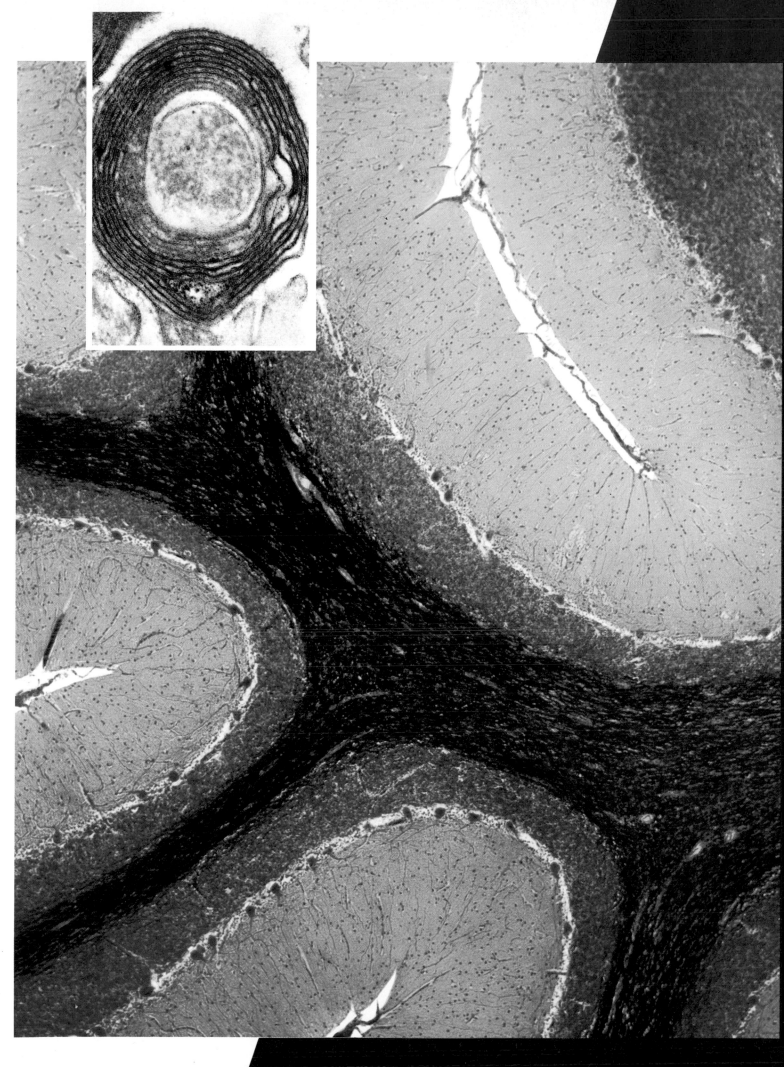

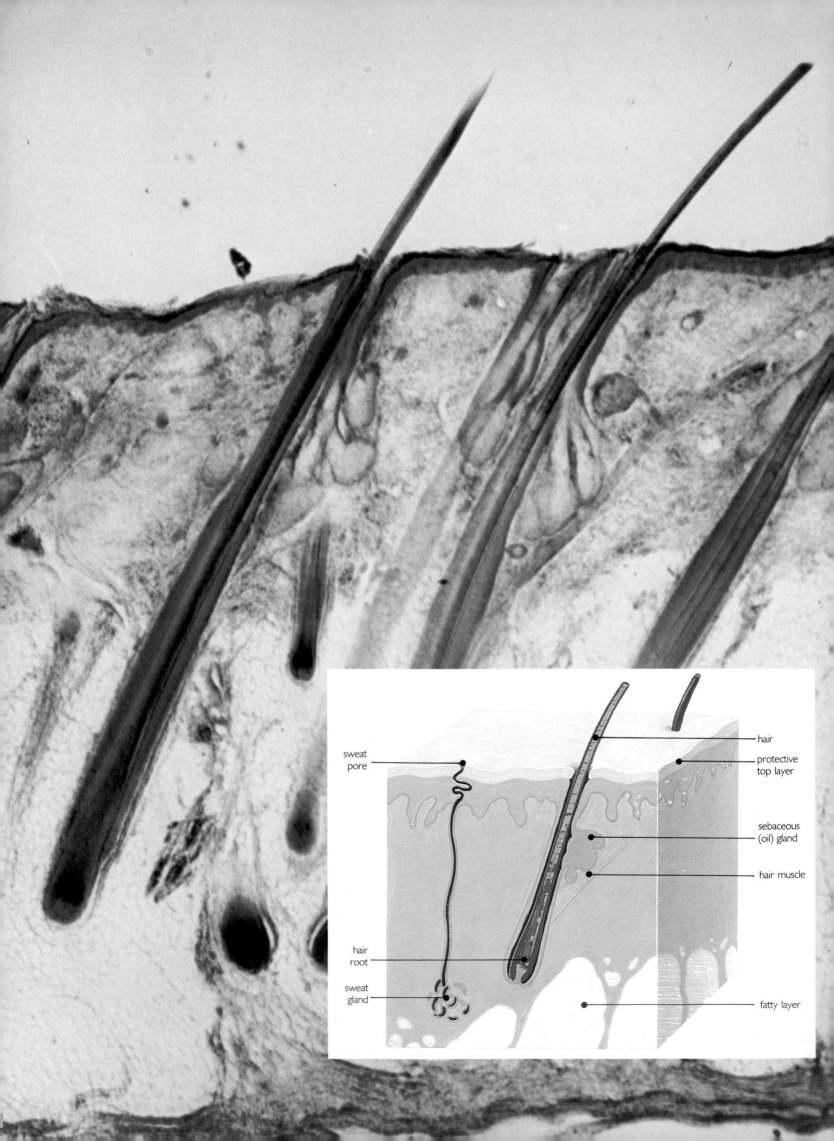

sweat
pore

hair

protective
top layer

sebaceous
(oil) gland

hair muscle

hair
root

sweat
gland

fatty layer

# BODY CELLS

Your body, like those of all large animals and plants, is made up of a huge number of living cells. Like blood cells (page 38), these cells are invisible to the naked eye, but are seen easily through a microscope.

You can quickly and painlessly obtain some of your own body cells by gently scraping the inside of your cheek with a teaspoon. Smear a little of the scraping very thinly onto a glass slide, then examine it through a microscope. The highly magnified cheek-surface cells you will see are rather transparent, roughly roundish and flat in shape – though many of them will be distorted into other shapes by the pressure of your spoon.

You may also see the nucleus of many of these living cells, like a large dot near the cell's centre. All human body cells have a nucleus, except the red blood cells.

◄Skin is the outer defense barrier of our bodies. It is also a main part of our heating and cooling system, helping to keep our bodies at a steady and safe temperature. In this photo-micrograph of a slice of skin, you can see several parts of its complicated structure quite clearly, and the diagram (**inset**) shows most of the remaining details. The protective top layer of cells, which flake off and are replaced continuously, keep nearly all types of harmful microbe out of the body. Sweat evaporating from skin pores takes heat away from the body to keep it cool. Fat deep down in the skin acts like a blanket to keep us warm in cold weather. (In animals, hair helps too, by trapping insulating air, but we have too little hair for this to count much.) Oil from sebaceous glands keeps skin smooth and supple.

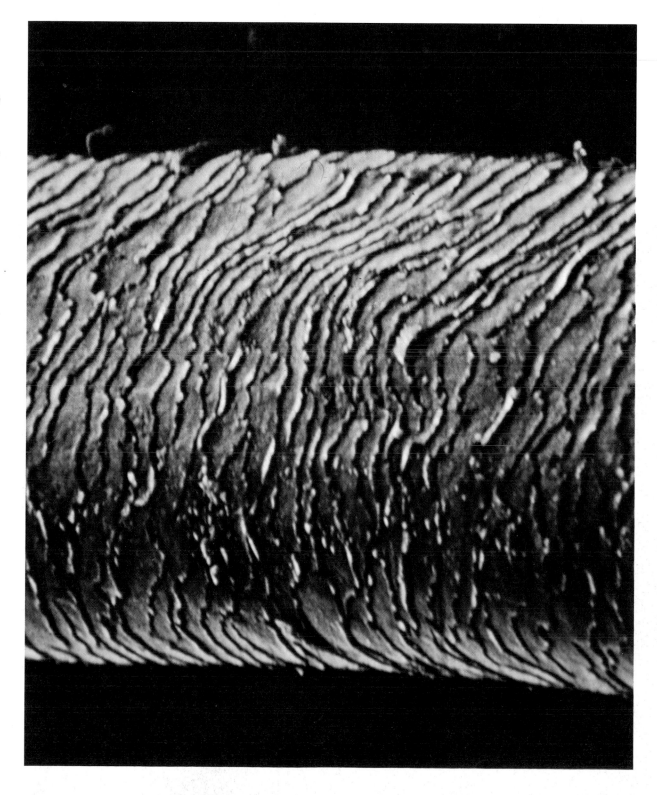

►Part of a hair magnified many thousands of times by the electron microscope.

# TISSUES AND ORGANS

►When you breathe in, air is drawn down your larynx and trachea into your bronchi, which then branch out into your lungs. The picture shows many of these structures but cannot show the parts where oxygen from the air is actually transferred to your blood, because these parts are microscopic in size.

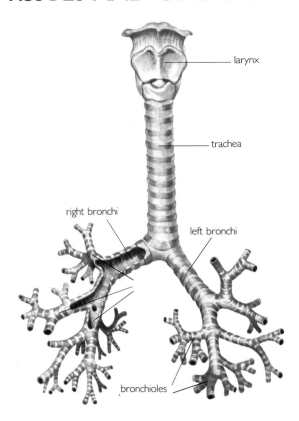

larynx

trachea

right bronchi

left bronchi

bronchioles

A body tissue is made up of many living cells all acting together. Bone, muscle and blood are examples of animal body tissues. Plant body tissues include the bark and deeper wood of twigs and tree trunks, and the green tissues of leaves.

Some of these tissues are easy to prepare to look at down the microscope. The thin skin from inside an onion shows many living plant cells. They are arranged more neatly in rows than most animal cells and, unlike animal cells, they have thick outside walls.

Animal body organs such as heart, lungs, liver, kidneys and brain are made up of various body tissues. These organs are, of course, big enough to be seen without magnification (unless they come from microscopic animals, page 22). But doctors and scientists study the cells of body organs under the microscope, for example in the diagnosis of disease.

▼This photomicrograph shows a bronchiole, a tiny air tube to the lungs. It leads to tiny air cavities, the alveoli. Beside the alveoli (but not in the picture) are microscopic lung capillaries, where oxygen from air breathed in enters the blood, and carbon dioxide from the blood passes into the lungs for breathing out.

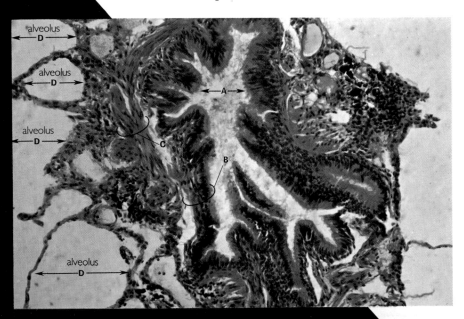

alveolus D

alveolus D

alveolus D

alveolus D

A

C

B

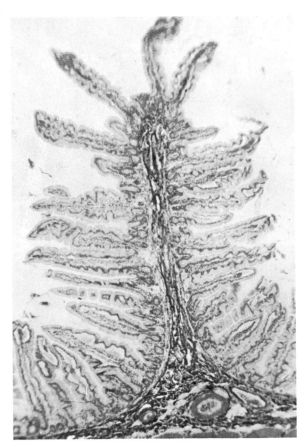

▲After being digested in your stomach and small intestine, food is absorbed into your blood through tiny finger-like villi in the intestine. The photomicrograph shows one villus. The red circles at the bottom are cross sections of small blood-vessels.

42

◀You may have seen the eyes of a cat glowing in car headlights or other light. Here, the same kind of glow can be seen in the eyes of a genet, about the same size as a domestic cat but related to mongooses and civets. The glow in the eyes of these, and many other, night-hunting animals, is due to the tapetum. This silvery layer in the eyes reflects light to produce the typical night-time glow. Like many other eye structures, the tapetum can be seen in detail only through a microscope.

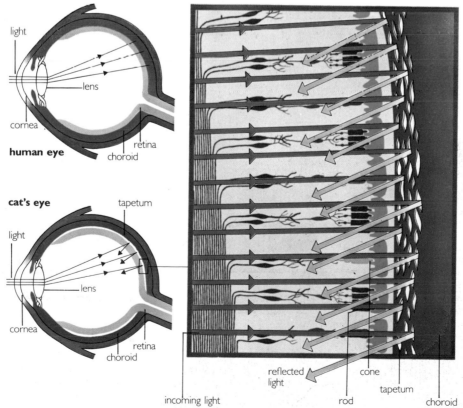

▶The diagrams show how light rays pass through the transparent cornea, or window of the eye, and then through the eye lens, to reach the retina which contains living cells sensitive to light and colour. You will notice the difference between the eye of the cat and that of the human. The light-reflecting layer, the tapetum, in the cat's eye, glows at night (**above**) if seen from directly in front of the eye.

light
lens
cornea
retina
choroid
**human eye**

**cat's eye**
tapetum
light
lens
cornea
retina
choroid

reflected light
cone
incoming light
rod
tapetum
choroid

◀In this diagram the retina of the cat's eye is highly magnified to show all its layers. The rods are living cells that detect light intensity. The less numerous cones are cells that detect colours. Both send electrical nerve messages to the cat's brain, to tell it what it is seeing. Some light, however, gets reflected from the tapetum, in the choroid or back layer of the eye.

# CHROMOSOMES, GENES AND SEX CELLS

▲Chromosomes only become visible when a cell is about to divide, as in this picture of a rabbit's cell. Then, the chromosomes show up as a tangled, tightly coiled mass of narrow threads. Each chromosome consists of an extremely long molecule of DNA, the 'chemical of heredity' bound together with protein molecules. If any one of the coiled chromosomes was stretched out straight, it would be too thin and faint to be seen except through an electron microscope.

As animals and plants grow, their bodies contain more and more living cells. A body cell multiplies by dividing to make two cells. The two cells then divide and multiply to make four cells – and so on. This process of multiplication and division is controlled by the cell nucleus – the roundish part of the cell, usually found somewhere towards its middle.

Inside the nucleus itself are the cell's *chromosomes*. These very tiny thread-like parts of the cell contain the even more microscopic *genes*. If the nucleus is the cell's headquarters, then the genes are the actual controllers. Everything that happens in a cell is directed and controlled by the cell's genes.

Most of our body cells have the same number of chromosomes, but some have only half this number. These are our sex cells – sperm cells if we are boys or men, eggs or ova if we are girls or women. When a man's sperm and a woman's egg come together, that is, when the sperm fertilizes the egg, the full number of cell chromosomes is restored. In a pregnant woman's body, the fertilized egg then divides and multiplies to make a baby.

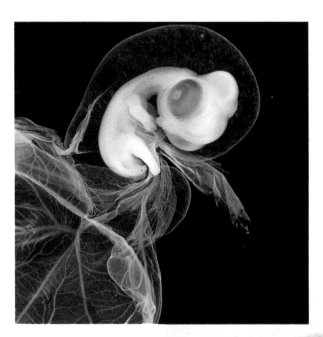

◄After a female egg has been fertilized by a male sperm, the fertilized egg divides and multiplies to form the embryo. The picture shows a 7-day chick embryo, enclosed in its membrane bag, called the amnion. At this stage the chick is about a millimeter long.

►Chromosomes are usually too small and thin to be seen in detail through the microscope, but these chromosomes are exceptions. They come from a cell of the salivary glands of a small fly or midge. They are much thicker and more visible than most chromosomes because each one is really a large number of the same chromosome lined up exactly side by side. Even single genes can be seen as bands of different thickness.

►When a female egg is fertilized by a male sperm, the nucleus of the sperm, containing its chromosomes, penetrates the egg to join or fuse with the egg's nucleus. Thus, the fertilized egg contains both the father's and the mother's chromosomes. This photomicrograph shows an egg just after fertilization. The sperm's tail, left outside the egg, is still just visible. The fertilized egg has already divided into two embryo cells.

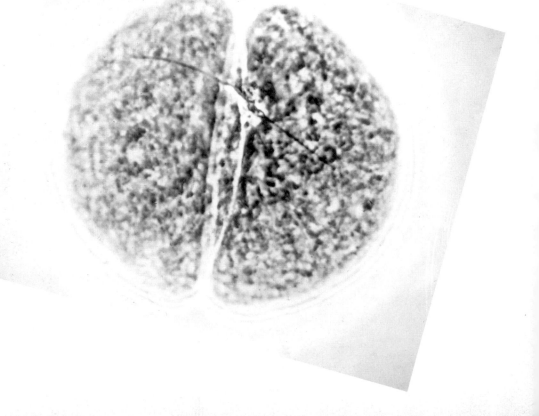

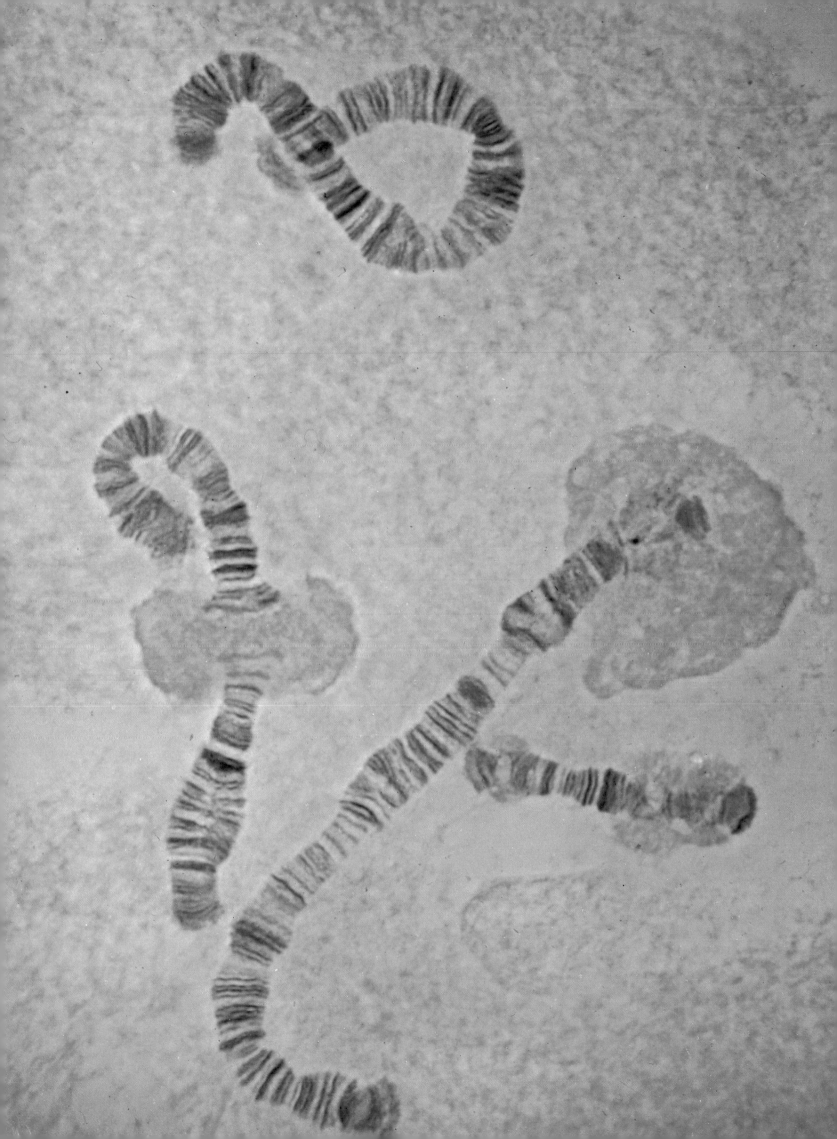

# GOOD AND BAD MICROBES

A microbe is any form of life that is too small to be visible without the use of a microscope. Microbes of one kind or another are about everywhere in the world. Some of the most useful microbes have been described earlier in this book. These include bacteria in the soil and fungi growing in and on wood. These perform the vitally useful task of rotting away the bodies of dead creatures and plants. The simpler substances so formed in the soil then pass into the roots of living plants, and help the plants grow.

**Harmful microbes**
These and other kinds of microbe are helpful and useful in nature, but other kinds are *parasites* that cause disease. A parasite lives in or on the living body of its *host*, a larger animal, plant or microbe, which it harms or even kills. Disease bacteria and fungi harm their hosts by growing in large numbers inside the host's body, where they may also make dangerous toxins or poisons.

Some protozoa or one-celled animals (pages 14 and 16) are parasites which also cause disease in this way. *Viruses* are

▼How the human body gets infected with disease microbes. There are many different kinds and they can enter the body by several different routes.

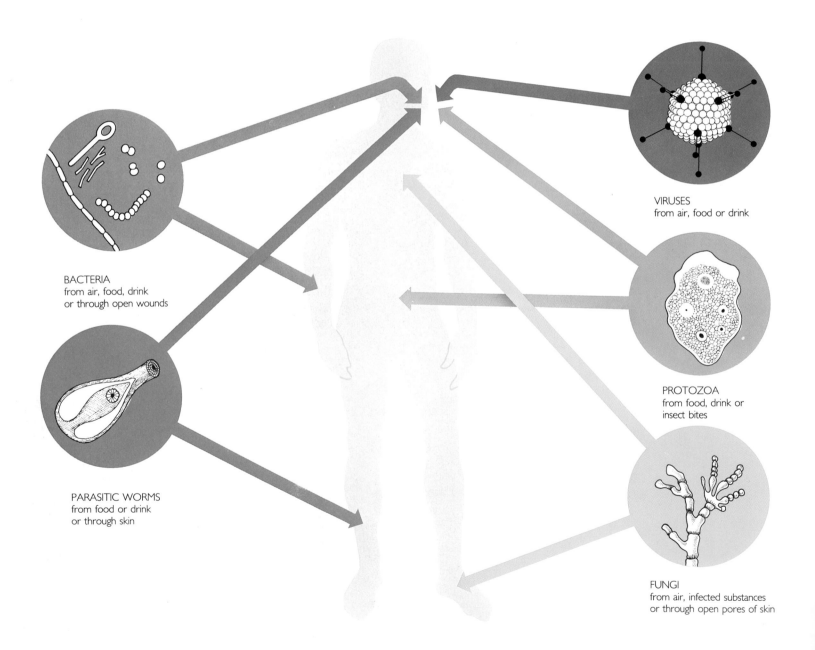

BACTERIA
from air, food, drink
or through open wounds

PARASITIC WORMS
from food or drink
or through skin

VIRUSES
from air, food or drink

PROTOZOA
from food, drink or
insect bites

FUNGI
from air, infected substances
or through open pores of skin

parasites even smaller than bacteria. These ultra-small microbes cause disease mainly by the damage they do to living cells.

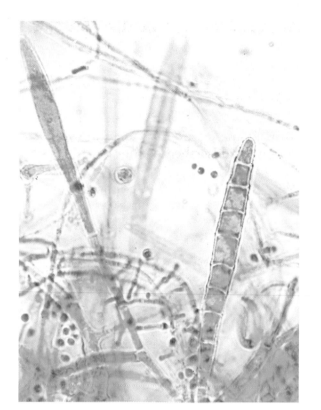

▲Marks on the skin caused by ringworm, a mild fungus disease. The picture (**left**) is a microscopic view of the ringworm fungus.

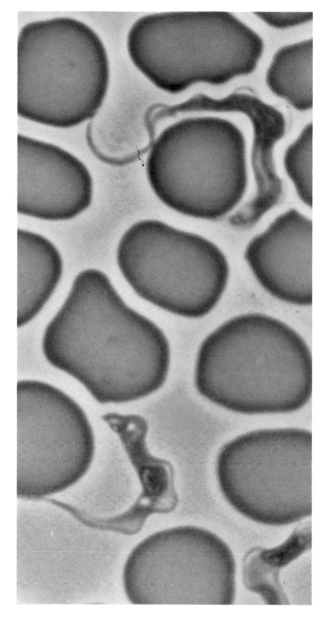

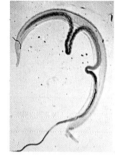

▲Bilharzia is one of human beings' greatest plagues. It is caused by this microscopic fluke which spends part of its life-cycle in a small water snail (**left**).

▲The deadly *trypanosomes* of sleeping sickness weave their way among blood cells of a sufferer. Sleeping sickness is transmitted by the tsetse fly, whose bite injects trypanosomes into animals and human beings. Not so long ago large areas of Africa were almost uninhabitable because the disease is fatal to tribesmen and their cattle. Better ways of combating the insect and the disease have reduced its destructive powers.

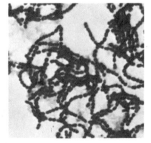

◄Sore throats are common illnesses. Very often the sore throat is caused by bacteria called streptococci. Under the microscope these appear as chains of dots or cocci (**above**).

# PLAGUES OF MICROBES

▼Malaria is one of the world's great scourges. It is caused by a protozoan, or one-celled animal, small enough to live in large numbers in human and mosquito cells. The malaria protozoan has a bewildering number of different forms, but the diagram shows how the parasite passes repeatedly between mosquitoes and human beings, so keeping up the infection.

You may have been unlucky enough to suffer recently from a bad cold. Colds are the commonest kind of infectious illness. They are caused by certain viruses, the ultra-small kinds of microbes. Colds are called infectious because other people will be infected, or affected, if you come into close contact with them. As you may know already, if you sneeze over someone while you are infectious they will probably get your cold. The virus is carried in the droplets of your sneeze, which the other person breathes in to become infected.

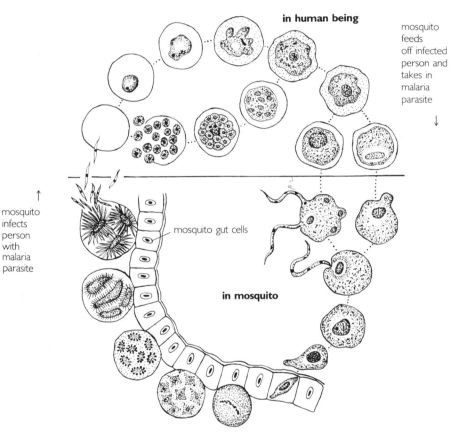

in human being

mosquito feeds off infected person and takes in malaria parasite

mosquito infects person with malaria parasite

mosquito gut cells

in mosquito

## Serious infections

You soon recover from a cold, but other infectious diseases can be more serious. Measles is another very common virus disease, but one that has more long-lasting effects. Many millions of children all over the world become ill with measles every year, and deaths occur in areas where children are severely undernourished.

Bacteria can also be the cause of dangerous infections. In past times, as the picture shows, bacteria caused world-wide plagues that killed a third or more of the people of many countries.

Carts full of dead to bury.

◀For more than 2000 years, history records attacks of pestilence or plague, that killed millions of people during each pandemic (international or worldwide *epidemic*). The Great Plague of London, 1664–65, although it killed one in every seven citizens, was only a small part of a more terrible European pandemic. Plague is caused by a bacterium called Yersinia pestis.

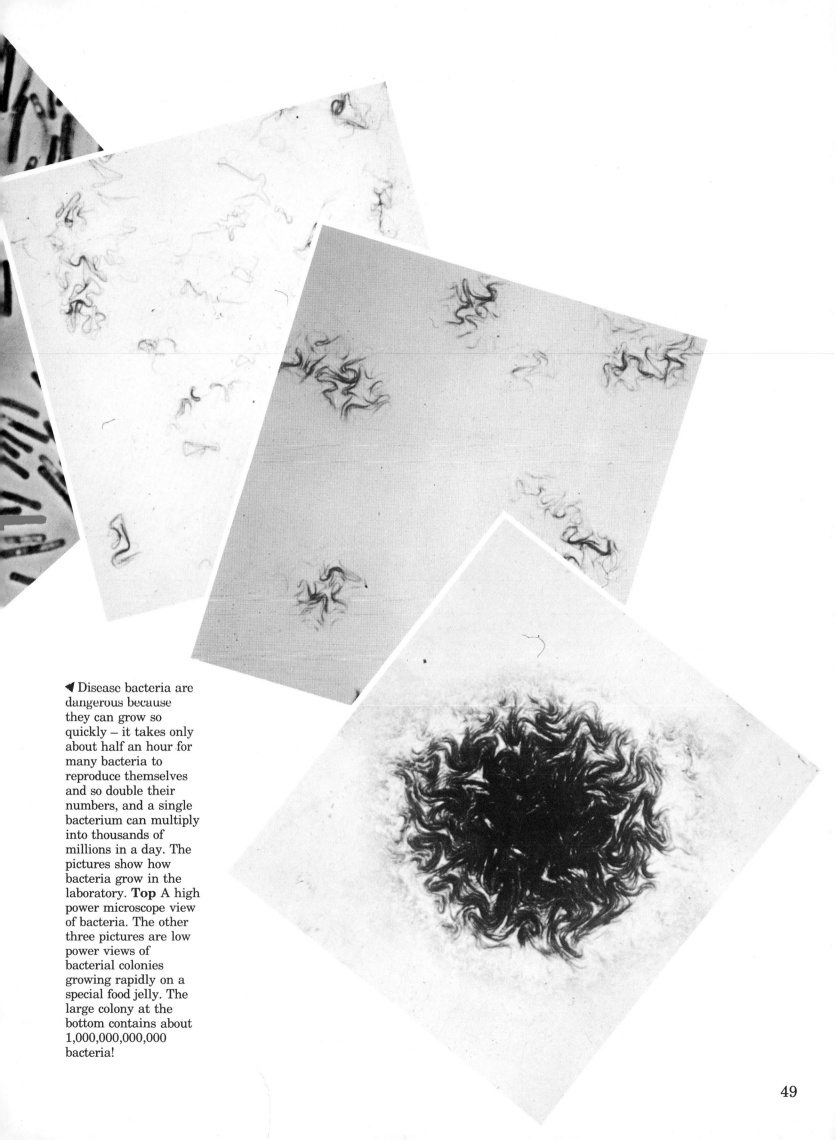

◀ Disease bacteria are dangerous because they can grow so quickly – it takes only about half an hour for many bacteria to reproduce themselves and so double their numbers, and a single bacterium can multiply into thousands of millions in a day. The pictures show how bacteria grow in the laboratory. **Top** A high power microscope view of bacteria. The other three pictures are low power views of bacterial colonies growing rapidly on a special food jelly. The large colony at the bottom contains about 1,000,000,000,000 bacteria!

49

# FIGHTING THE MICROBES

In the better-off parts of the world, infections caused by bacteria are not as widespread or as deadly as they were in the centuries of the great plagues. You might think this great improvement is the result of modern medical treatment and its wonder drugs. Really, though, it is more the result of healthier living conditions and better food. When people are healthy and well fed, they have a greater *resistance* to infections.

Unfortunately for the people of many undeveloped countries, modern medical treatment is not available, because it costs too much.

Worse still, these are the very countries in which living conditions are still very unhealthy and food is still very scanty and poor. Because of their bad living conditions, the people of these poorest countries have less resistance to infections and many bacterial diseases are still very common there.

▲Louis Pasteur (1822–95) was a famous microbiologist. He invented the process of *pasteurization* which rids milk of infectious bacteria. He also developed a vaccine against the dreaded virus disease rabies.

▶The apparatus used in making vaccines and other drugs is now very complicated. This machine handles hundreds of samples at once.

**Opposite** Like a scene from another world, this picture actually shows a white cell of the blood about to swallow up a group of harmful bacteria. The white cell, a phagocyte, wanders about in the body like an amoeba (page 17). The bacteria are called staphylococci, and cause boils and other infections. The picture was taken with an electron microscope at a magnification of about 20,000 times.

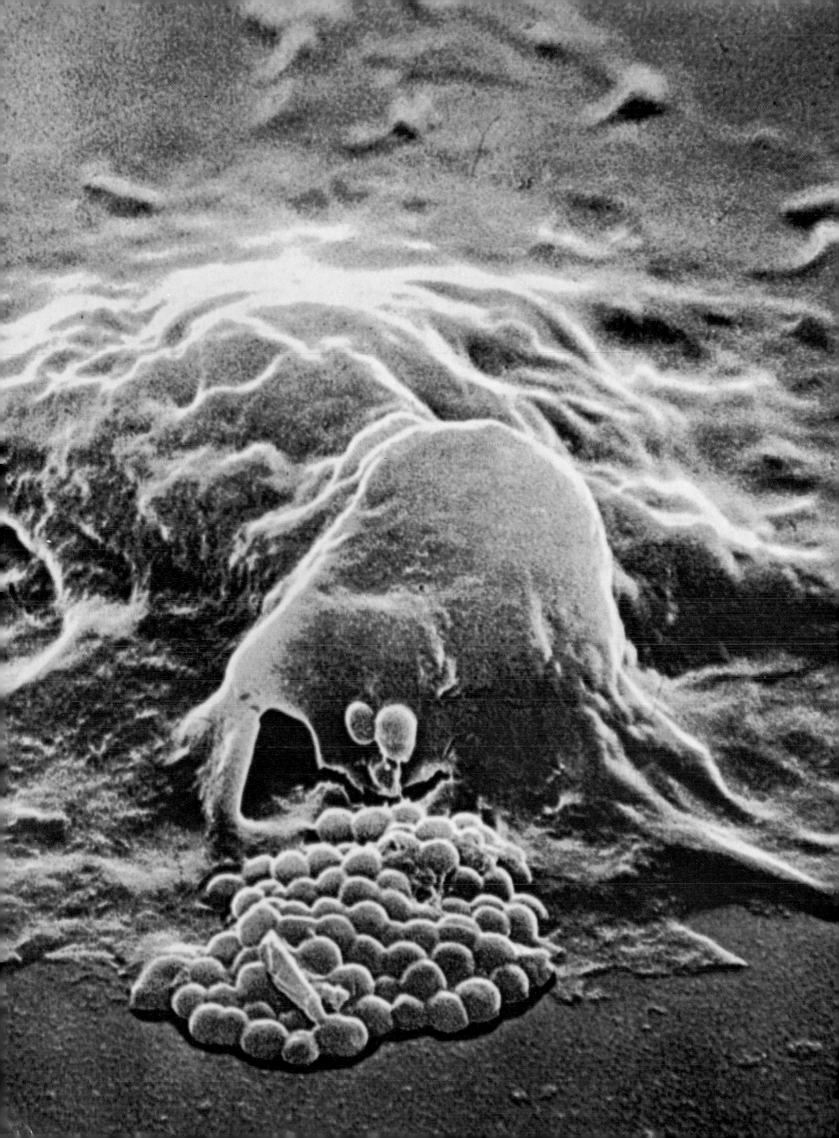

# MEDICAL DETECTIVES

The story of modern medicine is like a detective story because its greatest discoveries have come from following clues. And just as detectives in stories use magnifying glasses to follow clues, so medical detectives have used the microscope to follow theirs.

**Microbes, microscopes and disease**
Microbes were first seen and described in the seventeenth century by a Dutchman, Anton van Leeuwenhoek. He was the first person to make a microscope powerful enough to magnify bacteria until they could be seen. Although Leeuwenhoek's descriptions of microbes aroused great

▲The pictures show how disease bacteria are grown and identified in the microbiology lab.
1 A sample of infected material, perhaps from a patient's body, is 'streaked' on to a special jelly in a Petri dish. 2 Bacteria have fed off and multiplied on the jelly to make visible colonies. 3 Tiny samples of various colonies are picked off and transferred to growth tubes to be cultured separately. 4 Eventually, the various types of bacteria have been separated from one another into test tubes, and can be examined through the microscope to help in their identification, and the discovery of the 'culprit'.

interest, no-one connected microbes with disease. This discovery had to wait another 200 years, until the time of the great nineteenth-century bacteriologists Louis Pasteur and Robert Koch.

Pasteur followed the clue that bacteria could not just come from nowhere – although many people thought they did! Pasteur proved that, on the contrary, bacteria always come from somewhere, including peoples' bodies where they can cause disease.

Koch then went on to prove that particular bacteria cause particular diseases. This was like a detective discovering the true identity of the criminal. Once a 'criminal' bacterium had been identified, drugs and other germ-killers could be developed to attack it.

## More powerful microscopes

Microscopes are still used to make medical discoveries. They have been improved and made more powerful, so that even the smallest bacteria, fungi and protozoa (page 14) can be seen through them.

Doctors and medical scientists also regularly use microscopes to examine body cells and tissues. This is important because disease often causes minute changes in the cells and tissues, and by identifying these changes, a doctor may also be able to identify or diagnose the particular disease.

▲Microbiologists use a platinum wire loop, which never melts or rusts, to take samples of bacteria from colonies. Between samples the wire loop is sterilized in a gas burner flame. This kills any bacteria on the loop and stops contamination of further samples. In a few seconds the loop cools down ready for the next sample.

▶Two very different views of bacteria. **Far right** Bacteria in the mass – each of the streaky colonies on the agar plate contains thousands of millions of these living cells. **Right** Part of the cell of a single bacterium, magnified about 50,000 times. The tangled hairs projecting from this bacterial cell are the bacterium's flagella, which beat or wave to propel the bacterium along in its watery home.

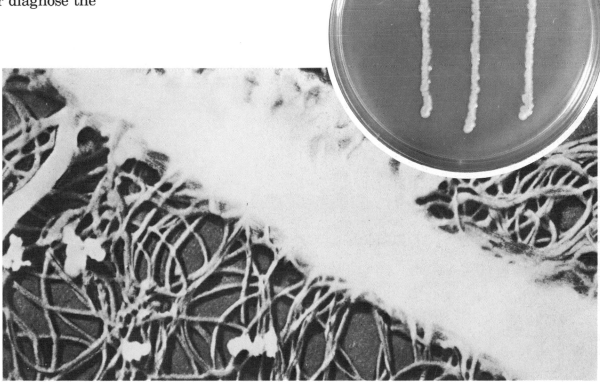

# THE GREATEST MAGNIFICATIONS

## THE ELECTRON MICROSCOPE

▲This scanning electron microscope can magnify from 10 to 200,000 times. Instead of looking down at the object through the microscope, you can see it magnified on the screen on the right of the microscope column.

►An electron microscope photograph of the tiny virus that causes the disease called polio.

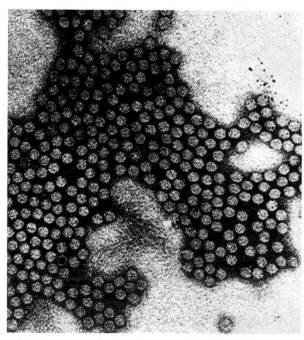

When you look at any object, you see it by light waves that travel from the object to your eyes. If you look down an ordinary school microscope, you also see objects by light waves, but this time the objects are magnified, perhaps as many as a thousand times. Most kinds of bacteria, for example, need to be magnified this much to become clearly visible.

What, though, if an object is smaller even than light waves? This is a real problem, because no such object is clearly visible through an ordinary light microscope. For this reason, even though the light microscope was invented almost 400 years ago, most viruses, smallest of all the microbes, remained invisible until 50 years ago.

At this time the electron microscope was invented. Instead of light waves, the electron microscope uses electron waves, which are far smaller and so can reveal far smaller objects. We cannot see directly by electron waves, but these waves are used to produce an image or picture on a screen as in a television.

With the electron microscope even the smallest viruses become visible, because these powerful instruments magnify half a million times or more.

►It is hard to guess what this is, but next time you go to the dentist look at the tray of instruments and you'll have the answer. The picture in fact shows a dentist's drill, magnified some thousands of times by the scanning electron microscope. This special electron microscope uses an extra beam of electrons. Its two electron beams are used to scan objects as we view objects by light with our two eyes. Just as we see in three dimensions, so does the scanning electron microscope — the dentist's drill looks not flat, but solid.

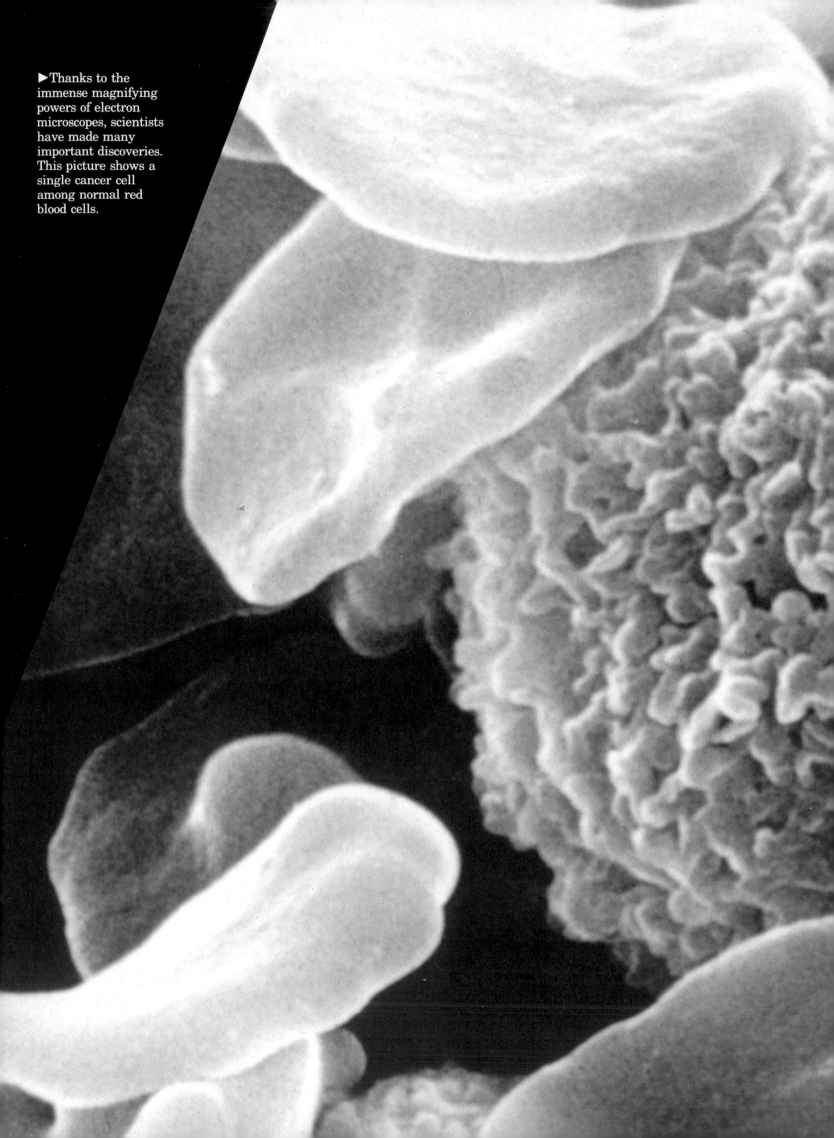

►Thanks to the immense magnifying powers of electron microscopes, scientists have made many important discoveries. This picture shows a single cancer cell among normal red blood cells.

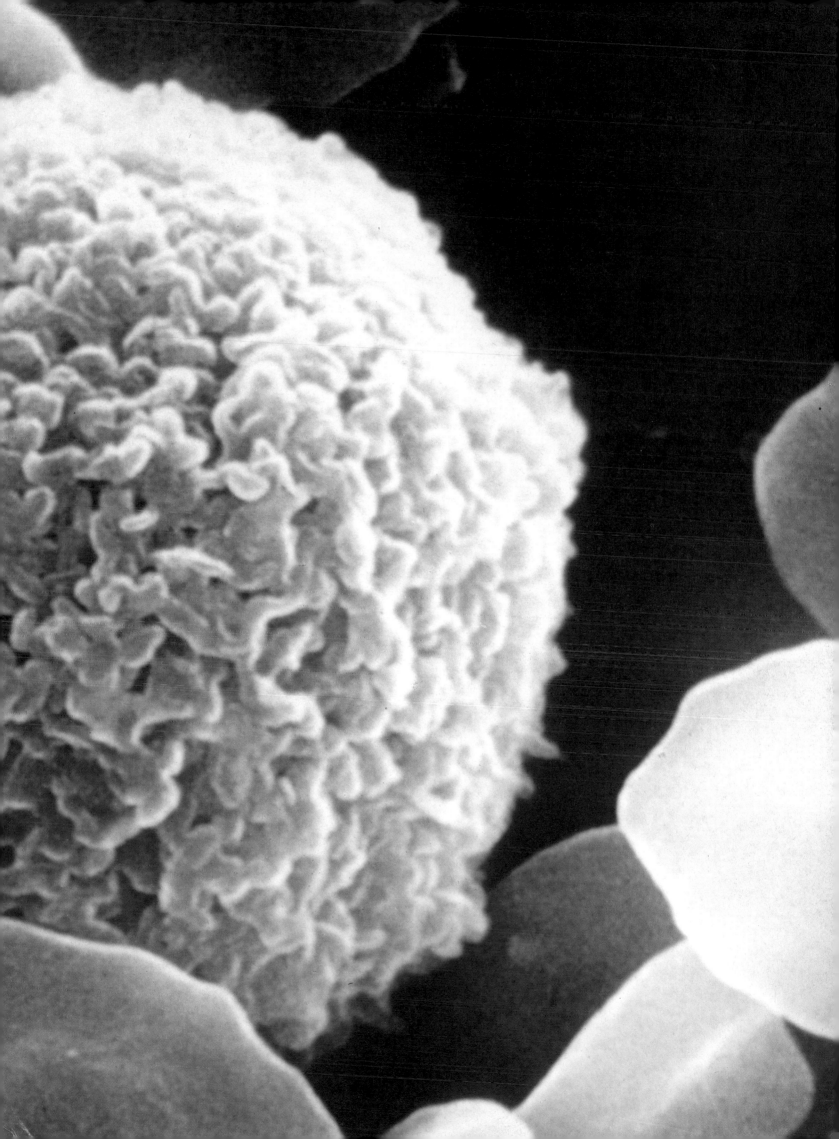

▲In the last century, the disease yellow fever threatened the life of anyone working in such tropical areas as Central and South America. This fever is caused by a virus, injected into people and also into forest monkeys, by the bite of the mosquito Aedes aegypti, an insect shown in a 19th-century drawing (**left**). The mosquito's larva (**far left**) lives in swampy areas such as the one **above**. Yellow fever is no longer such a plague thanks to modern insecticides.

Viruses are the smallest of all microbes. They are smaller even than the single-celled forms of life called bacteria. Unlike bacteria and other single-cell organisms such as protozoa (page 14), viruses are not living cells. So what are they?

## Made up of molecules

Any living cell, whether that of a microbe, a plant or an animal, is an immensely complicated system of life. You can think of a living cell as a microscopic factory that makes many different products, and is itself built of many different materials.

The products and materials of a cell are chemical molecules, the molecules of life. These are of many different kinds, and a living cell contains huge numbers of them.

Viruses, too, are made up of chemical molecules, but of many fewer numbers and kinds. That is, a virus is much simpler than a living cell. If a cell is like a factory, then a virus is more like a machine.

The way in which living cells are able to divide and multiply was described on page 44. Viruses, however, are too simple to do this alone. They need to enter living cells to reproduce and multiply themselves.

◀Scientists need to grow and study viruses, to find out more about the diseases they cause. But viruses will only grow and multiply inside living cells. So hen's eggs are often used to cultivate the viruses of 'flu, hepatitis and many other diseases. The *virologist* is shown testing a virus after it has been grown in egg cells.

▼Particles of hepatitis virus, magnified by the electron microscope. Hepatitis is a disease that strikes at many people – including careless tourists who do not boil their drinking water in countries where the water supply is not very safe. Injections of anti-serums, special substances developed by virologists (**left**), give protection against hepatitis.

# MAGNIFYING BY MILLIONS

A powerful light microscope will magnify more than a thousand times. An electron microscope can be 500 times more powerful still, so can make things look more than half a million times larger than they really are. At such magnifications, even the smallest objects and living organisms become visible. Yet many details of the world still remain invisible to us. It is almost as if the more we can see, the more there is to see!

**Seeing molecules and atoms**
All objects and living organisms are made out of chemical *molecules*. Only the largest of these molecules can be seen, even with the most powerful electron microscope.

▶Electron microscopes are the most powerful magnifiers generally used in science. In this electronmicrograph, a virus particle is magnified nearly a million times.

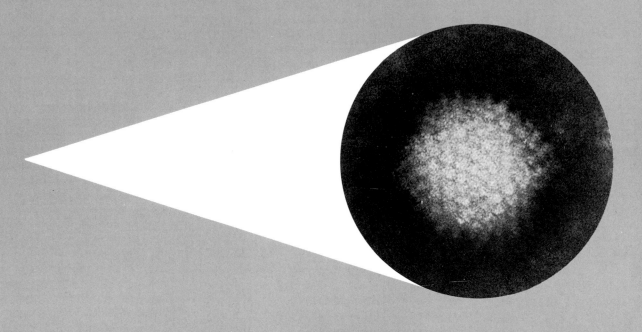

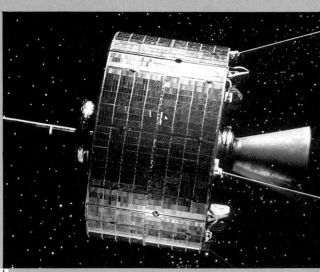

▶If a pencil 17.7 cm (7 in) long was magnified as much as the virus particle above, it would be about 160 km (100 miles) long and so, stood upright, would reach as far as the orbit of many a space satellite.

Molecules themselves are made out of *atoms*, which are the smallest parts of any material or substance. The largest and most complicated molecules contain a million or more atoms, the simplest molecules only one or two atoms. So how can anything as incredibly small as a simple molecule or an atom ever be seen?

Science has come up with answers to this question too. One answer is the field ion microscope, an instrument that can magnify metals several million times – making even their atoms visible.

The intriguing question now, of course, is what else will scientists discover with this microscope?

►Atoms are so small that not even the electron microscope can make them visible. With the new technique of field ion microscopy, however, some atoms can be seen. The picture shows metal atoms magnified in this way no fewer than 5 million times.

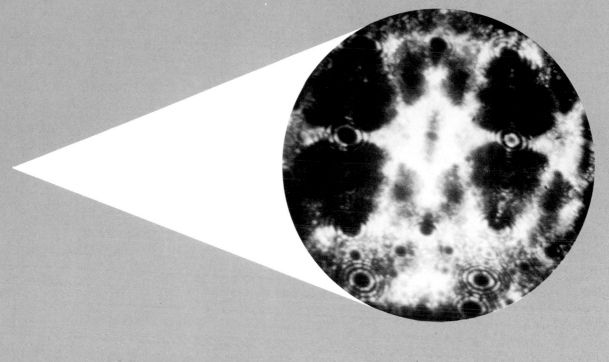

►If a beach ball 68 cm (27 in) across was magnified as much as the metal atoms above, the ball would be as big as the Moon – 3,476 km (2,160 miles) in diameter!

# GLOSSARY

**Alga** (plural **algae**) A simple green plant. There are many different kinds of alga, from microscopic single-cells to giant seaweeds.

**Alloys** Hard substances made up of one or more kinds of metal, sometimes with other, non-metallic substances added. Steel, brass and aluminum alloys are common examples.

**Atoms** The smallest parts of any substance or material. Atoms themselves are made up of still smaller particles such as electrons and protons but these are not usually called 'materials'.

**Axon** The long, thread-like part of a nerve cell.

**Bacteria** (singular **bacterium**) Microscopic single-celled forms of life. They are different from protozoa because they are an even simpler kind of living cell.

**Bacteriologist** A scientist who studies bacteria.

**Chlorophyll** The green pigment in plant leaves and stems, and in algae, that allows these plants to build up their own bodies from carbon dioxide gas and water, with the aid of sunlight.

**Chloroplasts** Microscopic 'packets' inside green plants, that contain the plants' chlorophyll.

**Chromosomes** Microscopic, thread-like structures inside the nucleus of all kinds of living cells (see also Genes).

**Cilia** Short hairs that stick out from many kinds of living cell. They are much finer than the hairs of your head and body (see also Flagellum).

**Ciliates** Protozoans with (usually) many cilia on their single cell. The beating movement of the cilia helps them swim fast through water.

**Crystals** The hardest and most 'ordered' of all substances. Their atoms are arranged in exact patterns, which give the crystals their beautifully regular shapes.

**Electronmicrograph** A picture of something microscopic in size, obtained with an electron microscope (see also Photomicrograph).

**Epidemic** A widespread disease infection, such as 'flu, measles, or, in times past, the deadlier plague and black death. Epidemics are caused by various kinds of disease microbes. When epidemics spread throughout many countries or the whole world, they are called pandemics.

**Filaments** Thread-like forms, such as those of many microscopic algae.

**Flagellum** (plural **flagella**) A long hair that sticks out from the cell of an alga or bacterium. By waving to-and-fro it propels the cell along. An alga's flagellum is very thin, but thicker than a bacterium's. Some algae and bacteria have a cell covered with many flagella, while others have only one or two.

**Fungi** (singular **fungus**) Living organisms in some ways like plants, except that they never contain the green pigment chlorophyll. Fungi range in size from mushrooms and toadstools which have large, many-celled bodies, down to microscopic, single-celled yeasts.

**Genes** Chemical substances which are a main part of the chromosomes inside all living cells. They are the chemicals of heredity. Each gene is a chemical 'instruction' which tells the cell what to do and what to make – including the making of another cell, or reproduction of the cell. Genes are what make us, and all other forms of life, exactly what we are.

**Host** Any creature or plant that suffers from the attack of a parasite.

**Marsupials** Pouched mammals, such as kangaroos, opossums and wombats. The pouch contains one or more milk teats which nourish the very tiny newborn animals until they grow big enough to look after themselves.

**Microbes** Any form of microscopic life. The main kinds are bacteria, algae, fungi, protozoa and viruses. Some many-celled animals are also tiny enough to be called microbes.

**Molecules** Groups of atoms which go to make up particular kinds of substances.

For example, the gas hydrogen has molecules composed simply of two hydrogen atoms linked together. Other molecules have several or many linked atoms, of the same kind or of different kinds. The complex substances of our bodies have molecules with hundreds or thousands of atoms, mostly of about six different kinds: carbon, oxygen, hydrogen, nitrogen, phosphorus and sulphur.

**Nucleus** The part of a living cell that contains the chromosomes. It is usually roundish in shape and found near the middle of the cell.

**Oozes** Thick layers on the sea bed formed from the bodies or shells of countless microscopic creatures which sink there when they die.

**Parasite** Any animal, plant or microbe that lives in or on the body of a larger living organism, and causes that organism harm.

**Pasteurization** Artificial process that frees milk of harmful bacteria, particularly those that cause the disease tuberculosis. The milk is heated briefly to kill the bacteria.

**Photomicrograph** A photograph taken through a microscope (see also Electronmicrograph).

**Pollination** The transfer of the male pollen cells to the female cells of a flower to produce the seeds or fruits from which the next generation of the plant will grow.

**Proboscis** (pro-bose-iss) The long tube-like or needle-like mouth-part by which many insects or other small creatures feed.

**Protoplasm** The liquid or jelly-like substance that is the main part of living cells.

**Protozoa** Microscopic, single-celled 'animals'. The cell is more complicated than that of a bacterium.

**Pseudopodia** Means 'false legs'. Amoebae are famous for moving about by extending parts of their cell as pseudopodia, then flowing into them.

**Resistance** In biology and medicine people, animals and plants are protected against disease by their resistance to attack by infectious microbes. A microbe, on the other hand, can become resistant to the drugs we use to kill it, and so survive to do us harm.

**Spicules** Tiny chalky, glassy or horn-like structures in the body of a sponge, which hold its soft tissues together.

**Stomata** Tiny holes on the surfaces of leaves and green stems of plants, which allow the passage of gases and water vapour in and out of the plants' bodies.

**Trypanosomes** Microscopic creatures with a single cell of a rather flame-like shape. Some kinds cause disease.

**Virologist** A scientist who studies viruses.

**Viruses** The smallest of all microbes. They are all parasites, because they need to penetrate living cells in order to reproduce themselves. They are the causes of most of the serious infectious diseases that we and our domestic animals suffer from. Viruses have structures that are much simpler than living cells. They are on the border between 'life' and 'non-life'.

►Brine shrimps are to be found swimming on their backs in salty pools. They are not really shrimps but are rather larger (though still very small) relatives of the microscopic water fleas such as daphnia shown on page 23.

# INDEX

**Acknowledgements**

Heather Angel,
Australian High
Commission, BBC
Hulton Picture Library,
C Bevilacqua,
C Bevilacqua/S Prato/
M Bavestrelli, Ron
Boardman, Paul Brierly,
Cambridge Scientific
Instruments, Camera
Press, C Castano,
H Chaumeton, N Cirani,
Bruce Coleman, Gene
Cox, Edefelt/Pasteur
Museum, Farmitalia,
U Fascio, Professor
D Fengel/Munich,
Giacomelli, Hughes
Aircraft Corporation,
IBM, Archivio IGDA,
Jacana, Luton and
Dunstable Hospital,
Mansell Collection,
A Margiocco, P Martini,
G Mazza, Dr McGregor,
Lennart Nilsson/Life
1970/© Time Inc,
Picturepoint, M Pitzurra,
Rassegna Medica,
Science Photo Library,
Siemens/Munich, Ron
Taylor, Transworld
Feature Syndicate,
Uniphoto, James Webb,
Wellcome Museum of
Medical Science, Zeiss/
London, Zeiss/
Oberkochen.